SECRET SPY
FROM
DRUMSHEE

CORA HARRISON

WOLFHOUND PRESS

Published in 2003 by

WOLFHOUND PRESS
An Imprint of Merlin Publishing
16 Upper Pembroke Street
Dublin 2
Ireland
Tel: +353 1 676 4373
Fax: +353 1 676 4368
publishing@merlin.ie
www.merlin-publishing.com

ISBN 0–86327–902–3

A CIP catalogue record for this book is available from the British Library.

10 9 8 7 6 5 4 3 2 1

Cover Design by Pierce Design, Co. Dublin
Typeset by Carrigboy Typesetting Services, Co. Cork
Printed and bound in Denmark, by Nørhaven Paperback A/S

SECRET SPY
FROM
DRUMSHEE

**Book 13 of the
Drumshee Timeline Series**

Cora Harrison taught primary-school children for twenty-five years before moving to a small farm in Kilfenora, Co. Clare. The farm includes an Iron Age fort, with the remains of a small castle inside it. The mysterious atmosphere of this ancient place gave Cora the idea for a series of historical novels tracing the survival of the ringfort through the centuries.

Other books in the Drumshee Timeline Series

For Ronan Kildea

Chapter One

'Daniel O'Connell is in deadly danger,' Mary Ann whispered to her twin brother. 'Don't say a word,' she added, and put her finger to her lips.

Ronan closed his eyes to show that he understood. There was no one but the two of them in the kitchen – and anyway, he thought with a chuckle, people didn't usually understand him, so it wouldn't matter what he said – but Mary Ann liked to be dramatic. She was always acting. She wanted to be an actress more than anything else in the world – to go on the stage like their aunt Caitriona over in France, to have hundreds of people clapping her, hundreds of people admiring her. When their father, Michael, went to see Daniel O'Connell in Dublin, he had visited the playhouses there and bought a thick book of all the plays by

William Shakespeare at a second-hand bookshop on the quays. Ever since then, Michael and Mary Ann, and sometimes Uncle John, had acted scenes from the plays every night in the little cottage at Drumshee, while Ronan sat in his special chair and laughed and cried and thought that each one that they did was the most wonderful play in the world.

Now Ronan looked at Mary Ann, his eyes full of expectation. Maybe in a minute she would get up and stalk around the kitchen; she would be the murderer with a knife in her hand, and then, a second later, she would be Daniel O'Connell, his long black cloak swinging free as he walked along, taking no notice of the murderer who was creeping after him with knife upraised. No matter what she did, Mary Ann could always get Ronan to see the vision in her mind.

But Mary Ann didn't get up. She continued dreamily stirring the pot of meat and vegetables that hung over the fire, on the old iron crane set in the chimney.

'Daniel O'Connell might get elected next week, Ronan,' she said. 'He wants to be a Member of Parliament – the first Catholic Member of Parliament. Da said that someone might get him killed before that happens. There have been threats already.'

Ronan nodded. Michael McMahon would do anything to protect Daniel O'Connell. From the time

2

that Ronan and Mary Ann were babies, their father had talked to them about Daniel O'Connell and how he was trying to make the lives of the Catholics in Ireland more fair, to give them the chance to vote. Now he was a candidate in the election for Member of Parliament for Clare. Someone would definitely have to protect Daniel O'Connell.

'Da,' Ronan said. 'Da' was one word that he could say very clearly. He didn't bother trying to drag any more words out of his throat. Mary Ann always knew what he meant. She could read his eyes; she had been talking for him ever since she had learnt to talk herself.

She glanced at him, knew what he was thinking, and shook her head violently. 'No,' she whispered, the word a hoarse growl in the silent, smoke-filled kitchen. 'No, not Da.'

Ronan looked at her in a puzzled way. *Surely Da is big and strong and tough enough to look after Daniel O'Connell*, he thought. His eyes flickered to the top of the dresser, just at the height where his father's head would reach, and then over to the gnarled blackthorn stick that stood in the corner beside the door.

'Oh, I know,' said Mary Ann impatiently. 'Da is big, and he's very strong, and he's very brave. If Da saw anyone attack Daniel O'Connell – even if there were ten of them – he'd be after them right away with his

stick, and probably have the ten of them lying on the
ground – like this.'

And she leapt out of her chair, spat on her hands,
seized an imaginary stick, whirled it around her head,
brought it down with a savage blow, stared in triumph at
the body on the ground and turned to face another
enemy – a little more trouble this time, but soon there
was another body on the floor. . . . Ronan laughed and
laughed and made cheering noises in his throat.
Sometimes he wished that he could be as big and strong
as his father; when he was younger he used to cry about
the fact that he could not walk or even move his arms
or legs. Now he was used to it, but he admired his father
very much and still wished that he could have been
born with a body that worked properly.

'Oh, Da would be fine for that,' panted Mary Ann,
going to the bowl of water on the windowsill and
splashing her hot cheeks. 'He's all right in a fight,' she
continued, tossing her curly dark hair out of her eyes
and coming back to sit by the fire. 'But you know what
he's like. He's always in a dream. He never notices
anything until it's right under his nose.'

Uncle John, thought Ronan. His eyes quickly flickered
over to where John's cap hung on the door.

'Not Uncle John,' said Mary Ann scornfully. 'You
know what he's like just now.'

4

He can't think about anything but Nora. Ronan glanced at the bunch of wild roses in the small jug on the dresser; Nora had put them there last Sunday.

'Yes,' agreed Mary Ann. 'Ever since he started going out with that Nora Dooley from Corofin, he's been as bad as Da. He just hangs around in a dream. Da says Uncle John and Nora are thinking of getting married next Easter, if she'll agree. Uncle John wants to get her away from that awful father of hers, who does nothing but drink, but she's worried about her mother and about Ned. Anyway, Uncle John's not interested in Daniel O'Connell, or in politics. He's just interested in farming.'

Just as well, thought Ronan. *It's a good job that one of the McMahon brothers is interested in farming.* Michael hated farming. He was always hoping to get enough money together to pay their passages on a ship over to France, so they could live near his sister Caitriona. Caitriona's sister-in-law, Aimée, had married a Frenchman who made furniture, and Michael dreamed of working at that. He was very clever with his hands.

Ronan glanced down at the special chair that his father had made him. Its frame was made from ash, and its seat and back from plaited willow shoots. It fitted him like a glove, supported his back and legs, and had two wheels attached to it so that he could be pushed every-where the rest of the family went. There was even a special tray that could be clipped onto the chair, so that Ronan had his own table for his meals. It was the best chair in the world, and his father had made it all by himself.

'You're right,' said Mary Ann, following the movement of his eyes. 'Da's great at carpentry, even if he's not much of a farmer compared to Uncle John. But neither of them would be much good at looking out for *spies*.' The last word came out as a sibilant hiss, and a thrill of excitement ran through Ronan and set his thin legs kicking against the chair. Mary Ann got out of her seat, replaced the soft leather shoe on his jerking left foot, and then sat back down and looked at him expectantly.

You?

Mary Ann would be excellent at looking out for spies – Ronan was sure of that. He could just imagine her hiding in doorways, creeping from shop door to shop door. . . . But Mary Ann was shaking her curly black head at him.

'Not me,' she whispered. 'I'm a bit giddy. I might start showing off, and then they'd notice me. Can't you guess who would be best?'

Ronan looked at her. He was puzzled. Usually he could guess what was in Mary Ann's mind as quickly as she guessed what was in his. Who was she thinking of? Who could be Daniel O'Connell's protector?

'You, of course!' she burst out, forgetting to whisper. 'You're very clever, you notice everything, you never forget a face, and you're nice and quiet. You're the one! You'll be the secret spy from Drumshee.'

Chapter Two

The next day was Sunday – Ronan's favourite day of the week. On Sundays, Michael always got him up early and dressed him in his best clothes. Then they all went to Mass. Ronan loved going to Mass in Corofin, meeting all the neighbours and watching their faces as they prayed and wondering about them; but best of all he liked what happened after Mass. That was when he and Michael collected money for Daniel O'Connell's fund, the Catholic Rent.

As soon as the priest finished the last prayer, Michael would wheel Ronan outside the church door and slot the wooden tray across his chair. Then he would put a wooden bowl on the tray. 'You all right, Ronan?' he would say; and then he would be off, talking to all the neighbours. Some of the poorer people gave a farthing a week, the better off gave a penny, but everyone on Michael's list paid their contribution.

This Sunday was an extra-special one. It was the first of July, 1828, the day before the election at Ennis, and Daniel O'Connell had promised that he would be at the church. As soon as they arrived in Corofin, Ronan could feel the excitement in the throngs of people waiting outside the church. Even Father Murphy himself, the parish priest, was standing outside, his white vestments blowing in the warm breeze.

Ronan looked at his father. *Where's Daniel O'Connell?* his eyes demanded.

'He's not here yet, Ronan. We're just in time to see him arrive. You'll see the pony and trap speeding down the road in a minute. Let's get you out and waiting for him.'

Michael stopped the cart, lifted Ronan down, placed him gently on the grass and then lifted down his chair. It only took a few minutes to do this, but Ronan was sweating with fear that Daniel O'Connell would arrive and he would be down on the grass behind all the people, not able to see him.

'He's not coming yet,' said Mary Ann, climbing on top of the stone wall behind him. 'I can see all down the road, and there's no sign of him.'

'Here we go now, Ronan,' said Michael, picking Ronan up. He was fastening him into his special chair when Mary Ann shouted, 'He's coming! I see a cloud of dust on the road.'

Quickly she reached up, broke off a branch of the beech tree overhead and waved it. 'Hurrah for Daniel O'Connell!' she shouted. In a moment all of the people around were breaking branches off the trees, or gathering handfuls of the red valerian flowers that grew on the walls, and waving them like banners and shouting.

Hurrah for Daniel O'Connell! Ronan's shout mingled with all the other shouts as the pony and trap pulled up in front of the church, just beside where Ronan was sitting. He was a big man, this Daniel O'Connell, thought Ronan; everything about him was big, except that he had a very small, rather turned-up nose. Ronan always noticed everything about people. The more he thought about it, the more he realised that maybe Mary Ann was right: maybe, even though he was stuck in his chair, he could use his eyes and ears to watch Daniel O'Connell's back. Nobody would ever suspect that someone as crippled as he was a spy.

He felt a thrill of excitement go through him as he thought about what he had to do. He carefully examined all the other men who had come with Daniel O'Connell. He would know them again, he decided. If he was going to find Daniel O'Connell's enemies, then he had to be sure who his friends were.

Michael left Ronan and Mary Ann and went forward to greet Daniel O'Connell, introduce him to Father Murphy and lead him and his party into the front seats in the church. Ronan was bursting with pride in his father. Michael was one of Daniel O'Connell's stewards, one of thousands all over the country who were organising the Catholics, parish by parish, county by county, to free themselves from the laws that stopped them having equal rights with others in the country.

'Come on, Ronan,' said Mary Ann, quickly seizing the back of his chair. 'We're going next.'

All the people stood back while Mary Ann pushed Ronan, just behind the priest, all the way up the church to his special place beside the altar, where he could see the priest as well as all of the people. Ronan saw Daniel O'Connell look at him, whisper to one of his friends and then smile over at him. Ronan smiled back. *I'm going to protect you*, he promised in his mind. *I'll watch you all the time we're in Ennis, and I'll make sure that no one sneaks up behind you with a knife.*

Ronan usually enjoyed Mass, the singing and the mutter of the priest's voice saying the Latin words, but today he found it very long. He wanted the day to be over quickly. The next day they would all go to Ennis and vote for Daniel O'Connell. At least, all the forty-shilling freeholders – the men who rented large farms

– would; the poorer people didn't have the right to vote. Michael McMahon was a forty-shilling freeholder, so he had a vote; and, which was more important, he was going to try to get all the other forty-shilling freeholders to vote for Daniel O'Connell.

As soon as the priest gave his blessing, Ronan looked at his father impatiently. This was when Michael usually pushed him outside to collect for the Catholic Rent Fund. Michael, however, was looking not at Ronan, but at Father Murphy. The priest had taken off his Mass vestments; he laid them on the altar and then stepped forward to the altar rails.

Suddenly a great silence fell on the church. A summer breeze blew in from the door – someone had already opened it, but no one stirred. Every eye was on the gaunt face and blazing dark eyes of Father Murphy.

He began to speak. Ronan felt as though he was at one of the playhouses his father had told him about. He could feel the excitement rising in the people in the church.

'Is there any man among you, any Catholic,' cried Father Murphy, 'any man who is mean and cowardly enough to vote for the landlord? Is there any man who can bring himself to do that when our hero, Daniel O'Connell, the Liberator – the man who will bring justice to all the Catholics here in Ireland – has put himself forward as your candidate? When he comes among us and asks for your vote, is there any one of you who can refuse?'

Ronan looked around the church. Every face seemed rigid with shock. What did those tight lips, those hooded eyes mean? he wondered. Beside him, he could feel Mary Ann stir with impatience. She always found it hard to be still for long. She was excited; he knew by the way her foot kept darting in and out from under the folds of her best Sunday dress. Her fingers played with the ribbons of her bonnet. Energy seemed to spark out from her, but still the people sat immovable – almost as if they didn't know what to think, what to do.

'Give me your word now,' shouted Father Murphy. His gaunt face was convulsed with passion; there were specks of froth on his lips, and his bony hand shook as he held it out to the people. 'Say the words: *I will vote for Daniel O'Connell!*'

Ronan looked around the church again. His small, thin body was almost jerking apart with the excitement of the moment. Everyone was staring at Father Murphy, everyone was shocked, but no one spoke; no one moved; no one had the courage to break the silence. Were they afraid? The landlord's bailiff was there in the church; he could end a lease and throw a family out on the road. Ronan looked at his father. Michael was glancing around the church; like the others, he looked as if he didn't know what to do.

Ronan made a superhuman effort. His body bent and twisted as he forced some air into his crumpled lungs. The words shot from him like an explosion.

'Vote for Daniel O'Connell!' he cried. He could hear the words in his mind; and, in his mind, they were as loud and as clear as Father Murphy's.

The effect on the little church was extraordinary. The shrill sound of Ronan's strangled sentence had hardly echoed against the high roof when every person was on his feet and a great shout went up from everyone.

'Vote for Daniel O'Connell,' they roared – as if all that great crowd of people had just one giant voice, Ronan thought.

Father Murphy stood in front of them, his arms spread out, like Jesus on his cross, his eyes burning with passion. Still the shouts continued. Mary Ann held one of Ronan's thin hands in her own and raised it up in a salute. Then Father Murphy lowered his arms and held one hand up for silence.

'Tomorrow I will be outside the church at eight o'clock in the morning,' he said. 'With the help of God, we will all go together to Ennis. But now there is one more word I will say to you. Already Ennis is full of soldiers and policemen. They are expecting trouble. If there is one hint of trouble, one fight, one drunken squabble, they will clear the town of people and none of you will be able to vote for Daniel O'Connell. I want every man in the church to come to the altar and give his pledge that no drink will pass his lips while he is in Ennis.'

'Bet Thady Dooley won't,' whispered Mary Ann to Ronan.

Ronan glanced down the church. Thady Dooley was the father of Nora, Uncle John's sweetheart. He was leaning over and whispering to his daughter; Nora had a worried look on her face and seemed to be arguing with him.

Ronan made up his mind instantly. 'Me out,' he said to Mary Ann.

'Not yet,' whispered Mary Ann. 'You won't need to start collecting until after everyone's taken the pledge.'

'Stupid,' said Ronan, his face becoming angry. He said 'stupid' more often to Mary Ann than to anyone else. The trouble was that he expected her to understand, and the rare times when she failed him filled him with rage.

'Me out first,' he said, with as much force as he could manage.

Mary Ann shrugged her shoulders. It was never any good arguing with Ronan; he was very stubborn, and if he didn't get his own way he might start having a fit from sheer frustration. She glanced across at her father, but he was busy whispering to Daniel O'Connell.

'Come on, then,' she said, and pushed her brother down the church.

The men had begun to throng the middle aisle, in order to come up to the altar and take the pledge, but they all stood back and allowed the twins to pass. Someone followed them, though, and when they reached the door of the church they saw that it was Thady Dooley. Mary Ann had been right, thought Ronan: Thady was going to try to get out of the church without taking the pledge. He would spoil everything for Daniel O'Connell by getting drunk in Ennis and giving the police and the army an excuse to send all the people away before they had time to vote.

'Stop,' he said, as soon as they reached the door.

'I'll just push you a bit further, Ronan,' said Mary Ann soothingly. 'You'll block the door if I leave you here.'

'Stupid!' he said. She looked at him in a puzzled way.

Ronan made a huge effort. 'Father Murphy,' he said. The words came out mangled and almost unrecognisable, but he looked at Thady Dooley and then fixed his eyes on Mary Ann, willing her to understand. *Tell him to go back; tell him Father Murphy said that no one was to leave the church until they've all taken the pledge*, said his eyes.

And this time Mary Ann didn't fail him. 'Oh, Mr Dooley,' she said, turning on her most winning smile, 'Father Murphy doesn't want anyone to leave the church until the pledge-taking is finished. He just doesn't want anyone to be hurt with some people going up the aisle and others coming down. Oh, and Mr Dooley,' she continued, with the fluency of a born actress, 'I wonder, would you help old Mr Doherty? His rheumatism is very bad. He'd like someone to help him up the aisle. That's very nice of you, Mr Dooley. He'll be very grateful. Mr Doherty, Mr Doherty!' Her piercing whisper sounded across the church. 'Mr Doherty, stay where you are. Mr Dooley is coming over to help you.'

Ronan watched as Thady Dooley, with a heavy frown on his face, went across the aisle and stretched out a reluctant arm to old Mr Doherty. He kept his eyes fixed on Thady until he had trudged up the aisle and steadied old Mr Doherty at the altar rail. It was only when Thady had given his own pledge to Father Murphy, kissing the cross the priest held out, that Ronan let out his breath. Hopefully Thady wouldn't drink for a few days after that.

Ronan turned back to Mary Ann. She was looking very pleased with herself. She always enjoyed acting a part; and the part of the sweet little girl was the one she liked best. Ronan chuckled. *Clever girl*, his eyes said as she looked down at him, and she gave a little skip of satisfaction.

'Time to start work, Ronan,' said Michael, pushing his way down the aisle. 'Come on, lad, you're blocking the doorway there. Here's the bowl. You should have a good collection today.'

It was a great collection. Person after person came up to Ronan and dropped a coin into the bowl on his tray. Some people who normally gave him a farthing gave a whole penny that day. Ronan kept note of them carefully. He would have to remember them: they didn't need to give any more for four weeks, if they didn't want to. One by one, Ronan sorted the coins, putting them into little drawers in his mind. Twelve pennies went into each drawer – that made one shilling. When he had twenty shillings, that would make a pound. The farthings had drawers of their own; his mind sorted them into little piles of four, forty-eight of them to make a shilling. He could see the drawers as clearly as he could see the little box that his father had at home for sorting the collection money.

'Here's Thady,' whispered Mary Ann.

Will he be annoyed? wondered Ronan; but Mary Ann had gone into action again. Quickly she leaned over, picked a small pink rosebud from the hedge and stuck it into Thady Dooley's buttonhole. She said nothing – just smiled, a sweet shy smile, into his face.

Thady patted her on the head. 'Aren't you the good little girl,' he said. 'There you are, looking after your poor unfortunate crippled brother, and you with no mammy to look after the pair of you.'

Mary Ann's smile became rather fixed. She hated people to call her brother a cripple. Ronan didn't care, himself; he thought most people outside his own family were stupid. He looked hard at Thady and then at the bowl on his tray.

'Oh, I was nearly forgetting,' Thady said, slapping his forehead. 'I owe you my farthing.' He took out a farthing, looked at it, put it back in his pocket again, and then, with the air of a lord, tossed a penny into the bowl.

'Oh, Mr Dooley!' breathed Mary Ann, her smile recovering its brightness. *How long will she be able to keep this up?* wondered Ronan.

But just then Thady saw his son Ned escaping with some of his friends from the village, and ran after him with a savage roar. Ned had to do all the work around the farm, while his father spent every penny in the public house. Ronan felt sorry for him, and for Nora; it would be terrible to have a father like that.

My da is the best da in the world, he thought, looking over to where the tall figure of Michael McMahon was deep in conversation with Daniel O'Connell. They were talking about the collection, Ronan thought; he could see both men's eyes on him. He strained his ears. He had great hearing, so he managed to catch the next sentence.

'You don't keep a list, then?' Daniel O'Connell was saying, and Ronan could hear the note of surprise in his voice.

'No,' said Michael, 'no need. Ronan has a mind as sharp as a knife. He never forgets anything. When we go home, he'll be able to tell me exactly who paid and what they paid.'

Both men seemed to realise that Ronan could hear them, and they came over to him.

'One pound, seven shillings, tuppence and three farthings,' said Ronan very quickly, and as clearly as he could manage. He wanted to show Daniel O'Connell how clever he was.

Michael bent down and sorted the coins into piles. Ronan didn't even bother to watch him. He knew he was right. He never made a mistake when he added up in his head.

'One pound, seven shillings and tuppence, three farthings,' said his father proudly. 'Exactly right, Ronan.'

'I'll have to employ you as my clerk when I go around to the law courts,' said Daniel O'Connell with a friendly smile. 'I could do with you. My present clerk is getting old, and he finds it hard to add up all the money.'

Ronan's eyes shone with excitement. He looked at Mary Ann and saw her smile mirroring his. *That will be a good job for me when I'm grown up*, his eyes told her. *I won't be able to farm, but I can check money.*

'I was just telling Mr O'Connell about you, Ronan,' said his father. 'I was telling him that if ever he wants a job well done, you're the man to do it for him.'

S410651

Chapter Three

onday morning started badly. Michael got Ronan out of bed, carried in hot water and placed him in the tin bath on the floor of their bedroom. He washed and dried him with his usual care; but when he started to dress him, Ronan knew that something was wrong.

'No,' he said, when he saw the old shirt and trousers. 'No!' *I must wear my best clothes to go to Ennis, to see Daniel O'Connell*. He looked intently at his father to make sure that Michael understood.

'Ronan,' said Michael, putting his arms around him, 'Ronan, it's pouring rain. I can't take you out in that. You'd get soaked. You'd catch a bad cold. John isn't going; you can stay at home with him. The ducklings might be going to hatch out today, and if they do, John will carry you out to see them. You'll have a great time with him.'

He thinks I'm a child, thought Ronan bitterly. *I'm not interested in ducklings*. 'But I have to go to Ennis,' he shouted. His voice rose. 'It's not fair!'

'What's the matter with him?' asked Mary Ann. She had heard Ronan's cries from her little room in the roof overhead. He had known she would come. Her feet had been on the ladder almost from his first shout.

'It's raining hard,' said Michael. 'I can't take Ronan. He'd get chilled and catch his death of cold.'

I must go, Ronan's eyes implored Mary Ann. *I want to see Daniel O'Connell. I have to look out for people who might try to murder him. You know I'm the secret spy from Drumshee.*

Mary Ann gave one look at her brother's furious face and one look at the soft summer rain streaming down the outside of the window.

'Never mind, Ronan,' she said. 'Stop shouting! The rain will be finished as soon as you've had your breakfast.'

She skipped out into the kitchen. Ronan's eyes followed her. He could hear her putting turf on the fire and stirring the porridge pot.

'Get him dressed, Da,' she called out.

Michael crossed the room to the clothes press, took out Ronan's Sunday clothes and dressed him in those, but Ronan hardly noticed. His father placed him in his chair, wheeled him into the kitchen, and seated him by the chimney. Mary Ann came over to him.

'The rain will be over after breakfast, Ronan,' she said calmly. 'I'll just tie this old towel around your neck, so you don't get your good clothes messed up, and then you can have your porridge.'

I don't really want any porridge, thought Ronan. He felt a little sick, but Mary Ann was standing over him with the spoon in her hand, and he didn't like to say no, in case they might leave him behind after all. Meekly he swallowed his porridge, spoonful by spoonful; then he sat looking at the sky, waiting, while the others had their breakfast. His father had no more appetite than he, he noticed. John noticed it too.

'For heaven's sake, eat your breakfast, Michael,' he said. 'What difference does it make to you if Daniel O'Connell becomes a Member of Parliament or not? What will Catholic Emancipation do for poor people like us – or for people like the Arkinses? At least we have some security, as long as we can manage to scrape together the money for the rent. They're tenants at will. They could be out on their ear tomorrow if it pleased the landlord's agent. What will Catholic Emancipation do for them, then?'

'Look,' said Ronan. His eyes were fixed on the sky. The soft rain continued to fall, but on the top edge of the Donoghues' hill was a small patch of blue.

'It's going to stop raining,' said Mary Ann. Her voice had no note of surprise in it.

'Do you know, I think she's right,' said John with amusement. 'Look, you can see the sun behind the clouds. I'll get the cart ready, and I'll put in that tarpaulin we use for covering the hay. You can always cover Ronan up with that if it rains again.'

And then everything started to happen. Mary Ann cleared away the dishes, washed them hastily with some water from the well and ran up the ladder to put on her Sunday dress, and John went out to harness the horse to the cart. Michael disappeared to the stone shed in the yard where he made chairs and tables for any of the neighbours who could afford them. Ronan's eyes followed his father. What was he doing? Michael had been out there last night, but there had been only a few minutes of sawing and no hammering. What had he been making?

In a moment he was back, carrying a small board. 'Look, Ronan, look what I've made for you.' He held up the board. It was beautifully cut, with rounded edges, and polished to a high shine. Cut into the board and carefully inked in were large black letters. They read: 'Please vote for Daniel O'Connell.'

25

'It will go onto your tray – see? I'll just slot it in,' said Michael proudly. 'Some of the people are making banners to carry, but yours will be the best of them all.'

'Mary Ann,' said Ronan.

'Mary Ann, come down. Ronan wants you to see his sign,' shouted Michael.

In a moment Mary Ann was down the ladder. 'I'm bringing my tin whistle,' she said; and then she saw the sign on Ronan's tray. 'Oh, Ronan, that's great!' she exclaimed.

Nice dress. Ronan knew he had to admire her first. Then he had to make her understand his plans.

'Ennis,' he forced out. *You take me all around the streets of Ennis, and everyone will see the board on my chair, and then they'll vote for Daniel O'Connell.*

Mary Ann nodded. 'Yes, we'll make sure that everyone in Ennis sees this.'

'The horse is harnessed,' shouted John. 'And the rain's completely stopped. Come and hold the horse's head, Mary Ann. Michael, you carry Ronan out. I've filled the bottom of the cart with lots of straw, so he'll be nice and comfortable. I'll bring out his chair and tie it to the back of the cart.'

And then they were going down the avenue, Michael leading the horse, Mary Ann dancing ahead playing her tin whistle, John shouting goodbye, and all the swallows swooping in the air so that Ronan thought they must be as excited as he was.

The journey to Corofin seemed quite short. More people joined them along the way, some in carts and some on foot. Ronan counted them off in his mind; yes, it looked as if every one of the forty-shilling freeholders would be there. Mary Ann began to play her tin whistle again, and soon everyone was singing.

At the crossroads near Corofin more people were waiting, among them Thady Dooley and his son Ned.

'Could I trouble you for a lift on the cart?' said Thady to Michael. 'My legs are tired today.'

'I'm sorry,' said Michael curtly. 'I have to pick up Father Murphy. He's going with us. I'm afraid I have no room.'

'So you're bringing that poor unfortunate crippled child with you,' said Thady, looking down into the cart. 'What's the good of that, in the name of God? He won't know what it's all about. Sure, why don't you leave him with Nora and the missus? They won't mind looking after him. I can easily sit on the straw where you have him now.'

'Stupid,' said Ronan. Probably Thady wouldn't understand him, but even if he did, Ronan didn't care. He looked at Mary Ann. *That stupid man doesn't know how important it is for me to get to Ennis. I have to look out for Daniel O'Connell's enemies.*

Mary Ann winked at him. She would probably have liked Ned to come, but she definitely wouldn't want that smelly old Thady in the cart with her.

'Sorry,' repeated Michael — but his voice didn't sound a bit sorry, thought Ronan, chuckling quietly. 'I'm afraid we have no room. We'll see you in Ennis.'

Mary Ann bent down towards Ronan, hiding her face from Thady, wriggled her ears and stuck out her tongue; then she straightened up and smiled, a sweet, sad, sympathetic smile, at Thady. Ronan chuckled again. He enjoyed the thought of Thady Dooley having to walk all the way to Ennis. *If he didn't spend all his money on drink,* he thought, *he'd be able to have a horse and a cart of his own.* After all, Thady was a forty-shilling freeholder, just like the McMahons.

'All right there, Ronan?' asked Michael. He sounded upset. He never really understood, the way Mary Ann did, that Ronan didn't mind what other people said. He always thought he was cleverer than they were anyway.

'Yes,' said Ronan.

'Good man,' said Michael. 'We'll soon be in Ennis, and then we'll put you in your chair and Mary Ann will push you around and show you all the sights.'

He shook the reins, and a few minutes later they were outside the priest's house waiting for Father Murphy. A great crowd of people had already gathered there, waving homemade banners or branches from the trees that lined the road.

'Mine,' said Ronan. *Show them the sign you made for my chair.*

'His sign, Da,' said Mary Ann impatiently.

Michael took the piece of board off the chair and held it up, and someone read it aloud. Then everyone started to cheer and to shout, 'Hurrah for Daniel O'Connell!' A few people shouted, 'Hurrah for Ronan McMahon!' Then the priest came out and the Corofin parish band started to play, and Mary Ann joined in with her tin whistle, and Ronan felt that this was the most exciting day of his life.

'We'll have to be very careful about the drink,' said Father Murphy as the cart moved off, the horse going at the walking pace of the lively crowd that followed.

'Well, they've all taken the pledge,' said Michael comfortably.

'A pledge is one thing; a thirsty man is another,' said Father Murphy grimly. 'Still, it's only for one day. I should be able to put the fear of God into them for that long, and all the other priests will do the same. Thank

God every priest in the whole of County Clare – except
for one misguided soul, that Father Coffey – is for
Daniel O'Connell!'

'Ned,' said Ronan to Mary Ann. *You'll have to get Ned
to keep an eye on his father*, he meant, but she misunder-
stood him.

'Never mind about Ned,' she said, tossing her curls,
her cheeks reddening a little. 'I don't care about him.
He's just a silly boy. I'm sure I can find a handsome rich
man in Ennis, and then I'll marry him. We'll build a big
house, with a special room for you, and we'll have lots
and lots of money and live happily for the rest of our
lives.'

'Stupid!' said Ronan. He would try again later; it was
easier for him to force words out when his chest was
held straight in his chair. Now he wanted to listen to
Father Murphy and his father talking about all the
soldiers and policemen in Ennis, and about how each
landlord would be standing there watching his tenants
vote. They would have to say their votes aloud –
Ronan was surprised about that, but it was something
that the landlords had insisted on, according to Father
Murphy. Of course, there were a lot of people who
couldn't read or write. It would take a lot of courage
for the forty-shilling freeholders to vote for Daniel

O'Connell. Nothing must be allowed to get in the way
of the splendid moment when Daniel O'Connell, an
Irish Catholic, would be voted in as Member of the
English Parliament for County Clare.

Chapter Four

'Now, this is the main square,' said Michael. 'Here's Ennis courthouse. I'm going to tether the horse down in the river meadows, and you can take Ronan around the town, Mary Ann. Look, there are three streets leading off the square. That one's Gaol Street, the one leading to the bridge is Church Street and that one is Mill Street. Are you listening, Mary Ann?'

But Mary Ann wasn't listening. Her eyes had gone to where Ned Dooley was lounging at the back of the crowd, trying to keep away from his father.

'Like Y,' said Ronan.

'Sorry, Ronan,' said Michael. 'What did you say?'

'Like Y,' said Ronan again. He looked at Mary Ann for help, but she had gone around to hold the horse's head while his father lifted down the chair.

'Grandmother,' he said with a great effort, as his father carried him down and fastened the soft leather straps around his chest to hold him safely to the chair.

'What's he saying, Mary Ann?' said Michael, taking the reins in his own hands.

The streets are like the letter Y, like Grandmother showed us when she was teaching us to read. He did his best to send his meaning to Mary Ann. He hadn't thought about his grandmother, Ann, for a while. She had looked after Ronan and Mary Ann, because their mother had died when the twins were born. Ronan had been left badly disabled after their difficult birth, but his grandmother had cared for him tenderly.

She had taught them both to read when they were five years old. He remembered her marking out the letters with an old knife on a piece of slate. 'A is for apple,' she had told them, 'B is for ball,' and so on until she came to the letter Y. 'Y is for you,' she had said, pointing straight at Ronan. Ronan always thought of that whenever he saw the letter Y. He missed his grandmother a lot, although it was four years since she had died. She had always given him the feeling that he was the cleverest, the most wonderful boy in the whole world.

'Streets Y,' he said impatiently. Mary Ann followed the direction of his eyes and understood.

'He says the streets are in the shape of the letter Y,' she explained to her father. 'Look – Church Street is the stem of the Y, the square is in the middle, and Gaol Street and Mill Street are the two arms at the top of the Y. We won't get lost, will we, Ronan? We'll remember that.'

'Clever boy,' said his father. 'You notice everything. Now, you two come back here at four o'clock – there's a clock up there on the courthouse. I should be finished voting by then, and we'll have something to eat and then go home.'

'Ned!' shouted Mary Ann. 'Ronan wants you to come around the town with us.'

No, I don't, thought Ronan impatiently. *Who wants stupid Ned?* Mary Ann liked him, though. He knew that. Ned was big and handsome and looked older than fourteen.

'Hello, Ronan,' said Ned, coming over and smiling at Mary Ann. He spoke in a very loud voice, as if Ronan were deaf. Ronan ignored him.

'Look,' he said to Mary Ann.

'What?' she said absent-mindedly, her attention on Ned.

'Look,' said Ronan again. She had begun to push his chair away from the square, so he made an effort.

'Daniel O'Connell,' he said. Even to him, the words sounded mangled, but by now Mary Ann was used to him saying those two words. She stopped instantly. All around them the busy, shuffling, restless crowd stopped also.

Down Church Street, there was a big building with a sign over its front door that said, in gold letters, 'Carmody's Hotel'. No one looked at the door, though. Everyone's eyes were fixed on a balcony above it. The balcony stuck out from a window; it was small, with only enough room for three or four people on it. It had iron railings, but every inch of them was covered with bunches of flowers and leaves, so that the balcony looked like a little garden. Behind the garden, a window had been opened.

Everyone held their breath – and then out onto the balcony stepped Daniel O'Connell. A great cheer went up; the crowd surged down the street, Mary Ann pushing Ronan's chair, Ned clearing the way in front of them. They only stopped when the great man raised his hand and began to speak.

Ronan didn't listen to the words. He was busy checking the men on the balcony with Daniel O'Connell. There were Mr Steele and Mr Shields – they had been at Corofin Church the day before. There was one other man there. Daniel O'Connell was talking about him – Gorman McMahon was his name – and flinging his arm around the man's shoulders. That was all right, then. Ronan memorised the man's appearance: reddish hair, turning grey; lines around his mouth; about the same size as Uncle John. He would know him again.

Carefully he looked around the whole crowd. He knew many of them already, the people from Corofin and Kilfenora. Soon he would know the others. He was confident of that. He had only to see a face once and he would know it again.

'I need lungs of brass and a tongue of iron,' shouted O'Connell. 'I have no words left in me. You all know what you must do now; so, in the name of God, do it. God bless you all.' He waved and turned to leave the platform.

And then the miracle happened. Suddenly he saw Ronan, there in his chair. The great man raised his hand and pointed at him. 'There you are,' he shouted over his shoulder. 'Read what Ronan McMahon is telling you to do.' And then everyone was thronging around Ronan and reading the words, 'Please Vote for Daniel O'Connell,' on the board in front of him. People were laughing and cheering, and bending down, and laughing again to see him laugh and to hear him say the words himself.

And then Daniel O'Connell went back into his hotel and everyone turned back into the square, and the people started to line up to vote. All around the square were small tents – booths, Ronan heard them called. Every man who had a vote could cast it there, but first they had to take a special oath. The queues hardly seemed to move over the next hour or so; this oath, which was full of long, strange words, took ages. Only when the men had taken the oath were they allowed to cast their votes.

Man after man, they said the name 'Daniel O'Connell' in loud, firm tones. Landlords stood around the booths, listening with furious faces as their tenants refused to follow their orders and vote for Vesey Fitzgerald. Ronan looked at these landlords very carefully. *Are they the ones who might try to kill Daniel O'Connell?* he wondered. He looked at Mary Ann, but she was busy giggling with Ned. She would be no good to him, he decided. He would have to manage on his own.

'Ronan, would you like to stay here and watch the people?' asked Mary Ann, bending over him with a winning smile. 'Ned and I are just going down to the fair in the new marketplace. Ned thinks it might be a bit rowdy for you down there – it's crammed, and there are lots of carts and rough men, he says. You'll be all right, won't you? We'll be back in a moment.'

Ronan made an impatient sound in his throat. His eyes were still fixed on the sour, long face of a landlord standing by the booth and watching his tenants voting for Daniel O'Connell. He hardly noticed Mary Ann and Ned leaving him.

There was a stir of excitement in the crowd. The door of Carmody's Hotel opened, and out came Daniel O'Connell and his three friends. They walked up Church Street and around the square, talking and joking with the patient queues of people. The three friends walked behind Daniel O'Connell, Ronan was pleased to see. That would make it hard for anyone to creep up and stick a knife in his back.

Then, above the noise of the voices, came the sound of marching feet. A gentleman on horseback rode into the square, followed by a line of men marching along. Each one of them was hanging his head, and Ronan thought they looked ashamed of themselves.

'Now, men,' shouted the gentleman. 'You know what you have to do. I'll be listening. Mr Vesey Fitzgerald is a good man. If that scoundrel O'Connell gets into Parliament, it will bring nothing but trouble to this unfortunate country.'

So he's a landlord, thought Ronan.

'Make way, there,' shouted the landlord, swinging his whip to open up a passage through the crowds.

Instantly everyone fell back, leaving Ronan, helpless in his chair, facing the angry man.

Yellow face, thought Ronan, *bloodshot eyes, shiny patch on the left side of your coat – yes, I'll know you again.* He felt no fear, not even when the man raised his whip again. He just concentrated on memorising this angry landlord's face and clothes.

'Coward,' shouted Daniel O'Connell, springing to Ronan's side and placing a gentle hand on his newly washed brown hair. 'Would you threaten an innocent, helpless child? This is the man who tells you how to vote,' he added, looking at the line of tenants. 'Would you trust this man to tell you the right thing to do? I wouldn't trust him to sweep horse-droppings off the street for me.'

The crowd on the square laughed, and then fell silent. Everyone looked at the line of tenants. Suddenly a voice came from the back of the line.

'Hurrah for Daniel O'Connell!' cried the voice.

'Who's that man?' shouted the landlord – but it was too late. All the other tenants took up the cry.

'Hurrah for Daniel O'Connell!' they shouted. 'We'll vote for you, Dan, you're a man of the people.'

'Let's bring you over to the hotel door, Ronan,' said Daniel O'Connell. 'Your father's gone on a message for me to the chapel up the town. You'll be safer there until he gets back, and you can keep an eye on everything for me.'

Carefully he pushed Ronan's chair over to the door. The people fell back and left a wide space for them to pass. Every face was smiling, Ronan noticed, though some of the women had tears in their eyes for some reason. He wasn't too interested in them, though. Suddenly he had realised that, while Ned was around, Mary Ann wouldn't be beside him all the time. How could he communicate with Daniel O'Connell if he didn't have her to put his thoughts into words?

When his chair was wedged into a gap between the window and the porch of the hotel, he made a supreme effort. 'You . . . danger . . . him?' he said, looking anxiously into the great man's face.

By some miracle, Daniel O'Connell understood.

'No, Ronan, there's no danger from him,' he said, laughing. 'That fellow would be afraid of a mouse.' Everyone around them laughed, and Ronan laughed too. He was happy now. Daniel O'Connell was one of the rare people who understood him. He would be able to warn him if danger threatened.

Chapter Five

It was over an hour before Michael returned, but Ronan wasn't bored or lonely. Many people greeted him – one old woman gave him a kiss, which embarrassed and annoyed him – but most of the time he just concentrated on watching the faces. He would know all the landlords again; he was sure of that. There was the unpleasant yellow-faced one who had threatened him, and the handsome one with cold eyes; those two were always whispering behind their hands together. There was the rat-faced one with the odd sideways walk – Ronan would definitely know that walk again, even if he couldn't see the man's face. Then there was the tall blond-haired one, and the small fat one with the greasy face; both of those looked harmless, but you never knew. By the time his father arrived, Ronan knew the faces in that crowd almost as well as he knew the hens in the farmyard back at Drumshee.

'Where's Mary Ann?' Michael sounded annoyed. Ronan turned his eyes towards Gaol Street, and luckily he spotted Mary Ann running down it, threading her way in and out through the crowds of people.

'I only left him for a moment, Da,' she murmured innocently.

Ronan stared at her hard. She knew he was looking at her, and her cheeks grew pink. He chuckled. She would be very nice to him for the rest of the day.

'Well, at least you left him in a nice safe place,' said Michael. 'Enjoying yourself, Ronan?'

'Daniel O'Connell,' said Ronan. 'Me.'

'Daniel O'Connell talked to you, did he?' beamed his father. 'Well, that's something that you'll remember all your life.'

'Are all the people going to have time to vote today, Da?' asked Mary Ann. 'It looks as if the queues have hardly moved since I . . . since you went away.' Again her cheeks reddened, and she avoided Ronan's teasing eyes.

Michael didn't notice the slip, though. 'You're right,' he said, with a worried look. 'They'll never do it all today. I'm going to see if I can line up the Corofin lads to vote.'

'I'll take Ronan down to the marketplace,' said Mary Ann. 'That was why I went down there a minute ago,' she added. 'Just to see if there was room for him. I ran all the way there and all the way back.'

Michael wasn't listening to her, but Mary Ann could never resist the opportunity to polish and re-polish her story so that it began to seem more and more likely. After a while, it would seem so real to her that she would begin to believe it herself.

The marketplace was full of people, but there was room to push Ronan around. Usually he would have loved it – the pedlars, the singers and the peep shows – but today he felt restless. He wanted to get back to the square and make sure that no harm came to Daniel O'Connell.

'Back,' he said to Mary Ann. Her eyes were fixed on Ned, who was across the marketplace, talking to some other girls.

'Daniel O'Connell,' said Ronan with a great effort.

'What?' asked Mary Ann absently.

Ronan tried again. 'Daniel O'Connell.' *Don't you remember? He's in deadly danger! I have to be the spy keeping an eye on him, making sure that no one sticks a knife in him.*

'Danger!' he shouted, so loudly that the people around glanced at him curiously and then looked away, as if embarrassed. Ronan didn't care. 'Danger,' he shouted again. The more he practised this word, the better. He was getting very good at saying 'Daniel O'Connell'.

'Oh, yes,' said Mary Ann hurriedly. Ronan relaxed. She knew what he meant. 'Ronan,' she continued, 'would you rather stay in the square with Da? He'll be queuing with all the rest of the people from Corofin and Kilfenora. Would you like that? You could keep an eye on everyone.' She bent down and whispered to him dramatically, 'And you could guard Daniel O'Connell from danger, couldn't you?'

'Yes,' said Ronan. He knew that she just wanted to go off with Ned, but he didn't care. For the first time in his life he felt that he had a job to do. It was lucky that he wasn't as silly and giddy as she was.

Once Ronan was back in the square, he fixed his eyes intently on Daniel O'Connell until the great man and his friends disappeared down Church Street and into Carmody's Hotel. *He's safe there*, thought Ronan. *His friends are still with him*.

He turned his attention to the queues in front of the booths. There seemed to be something happening there. A great murmur of anger rose from the crowd. A man had come out of a booth and was shouting something. Ronan strained his ears.

'Ye can all go home,' the man was shouting. 'There's not going to be time to register all the votes tonight. Ye can come back in the morning.'

'But some of these people have come thirty miles,' shouted Father Murphy. 'You can't turn them away now. There'll be daylight for another few hours. Can't you at least try to get the votes of the country people registered tonight? The people who live in Ennis can come back tomorrow.'

'Booths are closed,' shouted the man, completely ignoring the priest. 'Go home, all of ye.'

The angry murmur swelled. The crowd surged forward.

'There's going to be a fight,' breathed Mary Ann, suddenly reappearing beside Ronan. Ned, he was glad to see, wasn't with her. Then he realised what she had said. He looked at the angry crowd.

'No! No fight!' He forced the words out. *They mustn't be allowed to fight. Father Murphy said they weren't to fight.*

At that moment, the man in front of the booth seemed to realise what was happening. He took a whistle from his pocket and blew three short blasts. In an instant the square in front of the courthouse was filled with policemen, all swinging short batons.

'Friends,' came a shout from the balcony. Daniel O'Connell had appeared, a half-eaten sandwich in his hand. 'Remember your oath,' he thundered. 'No fighting, no drinking. Don't give them any excuse.'

'That's right,' said the polling officer. His bravery had come back with the presence of the police. 'Ye go off to your homes, now, like good lads. Let's have no trouble.'

'If they all go back to Kilrush and Kilkee and Killaloe and places like that, they'll never come back tomorrow,' whispered Mary Ann.

It almost seemed as if Daniel O'Connell had heard her, Ronan thought – or at least his mind worked the same way. Again he raised his magnificent voice.

'Don't go home, lads,' he shouted in his broad Kerry accent. 'Sure, it's a lovely evening. Why don't ye all go down to the meadows by the River Fergus and camp there for the night? I'll be down there meself in a while and see that ye're all comfortable.'

'Hurrah for Daniel O'Connell!' yelled everyone, and Ronan joined in as loudly as he could.

'Follow me,' shouted Father Murphy.

All of the people from Corofin and Kilfenora followed him out of the square, the voters from Kilrush joined in at the tail end of the procession, and then other priests began to marshal their parishioners and soon the square was half-empty. Michael came across and stood next to Ronan and Mary Ann. They watched intently while the square emptied. Everyone seemed in great good humour, and there was no sign of anyone slinking guiltily away. The people of Clare were determined to stay and register their votes for Daniel O'Connell, no matter how long it took.

'Michael,' said a voice behind them. Ronan turned around and saw Daniel O'Connell himself, still holding his half-eaten sandwich. 'Michael,' he said, 'we must get some food for those people and bring it down to the river meadows. John Steele has gone down to get some of the priests back, and we'll go around the town and into the hotels and collect money from the well-off.'

'Mr O'Connell,' said Michael in a low voice, 'I'm very sorry, but I must take the children home. I can't have the boy sleeping out in the open in the night mists. I'll be back before dawn, I promise you that.'

'No!' The word burst from both Mary Ann and Ronan, but Ronan's was louder.

'It'll be really upsetting for Ronan if you take him home Da,' said Mary Ann. 'He might even cry,' she added, with her usual cleverness at managing her soft-hearted father.

'No,' said Ronan violently. He looked at her with fury in his eyes. Was she trying to pretend he was a baby? He hadn't cried for years not in front of people, anyway.

'Me . . . you,' was all that he managed to say, but he fixed his large, intelligent eyes on Daniel O'Connell's face and tried to communicate with him. *I want to stay and keep an eye on you. I'm the secret spy from Drumshee. I know everyone now. I'll know if any stranger tries to get near you.*

Again, by some miracle, Daniel O'Connell seemed to understand some of what he meant. 'I can't do without Ronan,' he boomed. 'He's one of my workers. I need him. Jack,' he yelled, and a fat, red-faced man who was standing outside Carmody's Hotel came running up to them.

'Listen, Jack, this is Michael McMahon, one of my stewards, and this is Ronan.'

'And Mary Ann,' put in Mary Ann quickly.

'And Mary Ann,' completed Daniel O'Connell. 'Michael's worried about having the little fellow out all night. Is there any chance you could put them up in the hotel?'

Jack shook his head. 'I haven't a room to spare, your honour,' he said regretfully. He looked at Ronan sadly.

'You see, he mustn't get a cough,' explained Michael in a low voice to Daniel O'Connell. 'It's dangerous for him. I'd be scared to have him out at night with no shelter.'

'What about a stable?' asked Jack. 'I've got a great stable. It's warm – no draughts. They'd be fine there. We can put in a few extra bales of straw. They can come and have breakfast in the kitchen with myself and the wife.'

'That would be great!' said Michael, sounding relieved.

'Well, that's settled, then,' said Daniel O'Connell.

'Do you hear that, Ronan?' said Mary Ann with delight. 'You're going to be staying at the same hotel as Mr O'Connell and all the other gentlemen!'

'And in the meantime, Ronan,' continued Daniel O'Connell, 'you and I will go and collect some money for food from all those gentlemen who are just going in to dinner in Carmody's dining-room. Michael, you go down to the river meadows and tell the priests what I said. Mary Ann, you can come with Ronan and myself. That smile should be worth a few crown pieces.'

'Would you help in the kitchen, Mary Ann?' asked Michael. 'Just to say thank you to Mr Carmody. You could peel the potatoes or do some washing-up, couldn't you?'

'I'll help Mr Carmody with serving the dinners,' said Mary Ann decidedly. Ronan knew she hated peeling potatoes. 'I'd like to be a waitress. I like pretending to be someone different. Do you remember when we did that play you saw in Dublin, Da, and I was the maidservant? Could I dress up in one of those black dresses and white caps?' she appealed, turning to Jack Carmody with her best smile.

'We'll be glad of your help,' said Jack. 'Go into the kitchen, and tell my wife that I sent you. I'd better go in myself and start taking the orders. They'll all have great appetites.'

'Wait until they're halfway through their dinner, Mr O'Connell,' advised Mary Ann over her shoulder as she danced off towards the hotel. 'They'll be more generous then.'

Daniel O'Connell winked at Ronan. 'Bossy girl, your sister, isn't she?' he said in a friendly tone.

'Clever,' said Ronan, making a great effort to say the word clearly.

'You're right,' said Daniel O'Connell. 'You're a clever family. I've got a couple of lads at Clongowes Wood College up in County Kildare, and I pay a hundred pounds a year for their schooling – and I don't think they're as sharp as you at all.'

A hundred pounds a year for a school, thought Ronan. *If Da had a hundred pounds, we could all go over to France and live in a lovely sunny place; Da could make furniture, and I could help him to design it. I wouldn't let him waste it on schooling.*

He looked at Carmody's Hotel. A delicious smell of beef soup was floating out of the windows. He could hear the sounds of clinking cutlery, bursts of laughter and the popping of corks.

'We go,' said Ronan firmly. Daniel O'Connell seized the back of his chair and pushed him across the square and through the door of the hotel.

Chapter Six

The dining-room of Carmody's Hotel was full of gentlemen in black frock coats and striped trousers. There were fifteen tables, and each table had about six men sitting at it. *There are nearly a hundred people here*, thought Ronan, quickly adding the numbers up in his head. *We should get plenty of money to feed all the people camping down by the river meadows.*

'Bowl,' he said aloud. He fixed his eyes on Daniel O'Connell and then looked hard at a large, shallow silver bowl that sat on a cupboard against the wall. Once again, the great man instantly understood. He took the bowl from its shelf, placed it on Ronan's tray and then tapped the side of the bowl with a silver spoon. Instantly everyone stopped talking and turned around.

'Friends,' said Daniel O'Connell, 'they have delayed the voting, in the hope that all those honest fellows, the forty-shilling freeholders, will go home and not bother returning tomorrow. The freeholders are camped down in the river meadows by the Fergus, but very few of them have anything to eat. Will you be generous and give something so that food can be bought for them? Ronan and I will come around to the tables. If you can resist me, I'm sure you won't say no to him.'

With that, he started to push Ronan across the room.

'No,' said Ronan loudly, 'no . . . there.' He had noticed a fat, jolly-looking man, with a half-empty bottle of wine in front of him, at a nearby table. The first piece of money would be important, he knew. The rest would follow the first.

'We're coming to you first, Maurice,' said Daniel O'Connell, immediately understanding what was in Ronan's mind.

The jolly-looking man gave a big, booming laugh, pulled a leather wallet from his pocket, took out a crisp pound note and placed it in the silver bowl. The next man had a half-crown ready in his hand, but when he saw the pound note he changed his mind and gave a five-shilling piece.

Around the room they went, collecting notes and coins. Ronan opened a new set of drawers in his mind: one for half-crowns, eight of them to make a pound; one for five-shilling pieces, four to the pound; one for ten-shilling notes, two to the pound; and one for the pound notes. The pound notes would bring the sum of money up very quickly.

While he was going around the room, Mary Ann came in with a basket of bread rolls. Ronan gave her a smile, though he didn't allow her to distract his mind from checking and counting the money. Her eyes widened when she saw the beautiful silver bowl and all the money lying in it; but, like Ronan, she allowed nothing to distract her from the part she was playing. From table to table she went, smiling shyly and dropping little curtseys. One gentleman patted her curls and slipped a silver sixpence into her hand, Ronan noticed. Then another gentleman did the same thing. *Five of those would make half a crown*, thought Ronan. *I hope she gives it to Da to add to the going-to-France moneybox.*

Michael came in just as Ronan finished going around the last table. Ronan ignored him. He was quickly checking through the drawers in his mind. He wanted to do it before John Steele, Daniel O'Connell's friend, had time to count the money.

'Ninety-seven pounds, eighteen shillings and sixpence,' he said quickly, while John Steele was still making little piles of the half-crowns. The words weren't as clear as he wanted them to be; he was getting tired and had slumped down in his chair. John Steele smiled at him, but Ronan knew that he didn't understand. *Tell them*, his eyes implored Mary Ann.

'Ronan says it comes to ninety-seven pounds, eighteen shillings and sixpence,' she said, so clearly that everyone in the room stopped chattering and every spoon was held suspended in the air. Every eye turned to John Steele, who was still piling the coins and notes into little stacks.

'Ninety-seven pounds, eighteen shillings and six-pence,' he said, after a long few minutes. He gazed at Ronan with an expression of such astonishment that Ronan started to chuckle.

'Sure, John, you were a long time over that,' joked Daniel O'Connell. 'I'll have to give you the sack and take on Ronan instead.'

Everyone in the room started to laugh, and then the voice of the man called Maurice boomed over the laughter. 'I'll make that up to a hundred pounds for you, Dan,' he said.

'Two pounds, one and sixpence,' said Ronan quickly, and this time Mary Ann instantly echoed his words.

'You've got a great brain, son,' said Daniel O'Connell. Ronan saw his father's proud smile stretch almost from ear to ear.

'Da. Look,' he said, directing his eyes at the cupboard where Jack Carmody was replacing the bowl.

'Yes, it's beautiful,' said Michael, following Ronan's eyes. 'That's a lovely cupboard. It's made of oak, isn't it?'

'It dates from my grandfather's time,' said Jack Carmody. 'I used to have another one to match it, there on the opposite side of the room, but a gentleman left a pipe burning on top of it and the whole cupboard went on fire.'

'I could make you a copy to replace it, if you like,' offered Michael. 'I have a lot of oak at home. We had some old oak trees – they must have been about five hundred years old – on the avenue; they blew down six or seven years ago. My brother and I sawed them into planks. The wood is nicely seasoned now.'

'That would be great,' said Jack Carmody. 'I'd give you a good price for it. We'll talk about it tomorrow.'

Ronan smiled sleepily. That would be more money for the going-to-France box. He would have to look very carefully at the cupboard, so that he could help his father by remembering every little detail of it; but he suddenly felt dead tired.

Jack noticed it. 'Why don't you put the lad on the sofa in the little reading-room across the hall?' he said. 'No one will be going in there for a few hours yet. I just keep the daily newspapers in there. He can lie on the sofa and sleep. He'll be as safe as houses there. Leave the door a little open, so he can call out if he wants anything. Give him something to eat first.'

But Ronan didn't want anything to eat. His eyes were closing. He swallowed a little milk, to satisfy his father, and then shook his head firmly. He hardly noticed when he was lifted onto the sofa and some chairs were placed in front of it to stop him rolling off. He was asleep before Michael tiptoed out of the room, leaving the door a crack open.

★ ★ ★

It was dark when Ronan woke up. For a moment he didn't know where he was; all he could see was a faint crack of light coming through the window, where the curtains met in the centre. Then he heard voices and laughter, and a smell of tobacco smoke came to his nostrils. He was at Carmody's Hotel, in the reading-room. But someone had shut the door to the hallway. Ronan had always hated the dark; he was terrified of it.

He was just about to call out when a voice spoke, so near to him that he almost jumped out of his skin.

'Smith will be able to do it,' said the voice. 'He's the fastest man with a knife I've ever known.'

'You're sure he'll be able to get near to him?' asked another voice.

The first voice chuckled – a nasty, evil sound, Ronan thought. 'In that disguise, why should anyone suspect him?' The words were a low, menacing whisper. 'He has his instructions. No need to do anything if the vote goes against Daniel O'Connell; but if he is elected, Smith has to slide the knife through his ribs and then make his escape instantly. Let's get back to those drunken fools. Wait – I'll just peep out and check that no one is in the hall.'

In an instant they were both gone, leaving the door slightly open. Ronan lay there. He no longer wanted to call Mary Ann. He wanted to think about what he had heard.

So Mary Ann had been right: Daniel O'Connell was in deadly danger. Ronan had not really completely believed her; it had been like one of the games that they had played together all their lives. For a moment Ronan felt panicky. Should he talk to his father? But then, that mightn't work. How could Michael find out who Smith was? *No*, decided Ronan, *I've more brains than any of them and no one will suspect me.*

He relaxed and set himself to work out the problem. What disguise was the murderer going to use? It must be something special. Ronan decided he would have to check everyone around Daniel O'Connell all the time and see whether there were any strange faces. Everyone who stood near Daniel O'Connell on the balcony, or on the platform outside the courthouse, would be well known.

At that moment, the door was pushed open. A gleam of yellow from the oil lamps in the hall outside shone into the room, and by its light Ronan saw an animal – a dog, but no ordinary dog like the ones that ran around the farms and herded the sheep and the cattle. This dog was huge, the size of a young calf. It gave a loud bark, hurled itself across the room, knocking over a chair, and threw itself on Ronan.

Ronan screamed. His screams were so loud that they even frightened him. The weight of the huge dog was pressing down on him; its hot breath was on his cheek.

'Ronan!' cried Mary Ann, running in, pushing the door wide open. 'Ronan, it's all right.'

'That's just Bruno, Ronan,' boomed Jack Carmody, following Mary Ann into the room. 'Get down, Bruno. You're frightening the lad. Don't worry, Ronan; Bruno is very friendly. He's a St Bernard dog, and they love people. He just wanted to say hello. Give me your hand. There, Bruno – gently, now! Just give him a little lick.'

The big dog licked Ronan's hand, a warm, tickly lick, and Ronan relaxed, although spasms still continued to rack his thin body. Mary Ann knelt down and put her arms around him.

'He's a very friendly dog,' continued Jack, looking anxiously down at Ronan's white face. 'He's clever, too. Wait a minute – I'll show you some of his tricks. Let's put you sitting up first; you'll feel better then. I'll light the lamp, too. Nothing like the dark to give people nightmares.'

Jack's strong arms lifted Ronan and propped him up with plenty of velvet cushions at his back.

'Now,' continued Jack, 'I'll go out into the hallway, and you just say, "Find Jack," and see what happens.'

Jack held up his hand briefly to the dog, and then went out of the room and down the hallway, his heavy footsteps making the floorboards creak.

Ronan looked dubiously at Bruno, and Bruno looked back at him with big, soft brown eyes. *He looks a bit sad*, thought Ronan. *Maybe he's upset because I screamed*. He smiled, and Bruno wagged his tail.

'Find Jack,' said Ronan, as clearly as he could manage.

Bruno jumped up and padded out of the room. A minute later he was back, his magnificent set of white teeth holding the cuff of Jack's coat and pulling him along. Jack was pretending to try to escape, but the big dog pulled him steadily across the room until he brought him right up beside Ronan.

'Now we'll try Mary Ann,' said Jack. 'Here, Bruno, this is Mary Ann. Mary Ann, you give him this biscuit while Ronan says your name.'

'Mary Ann,' said Ronan firmly, while Mary Ann gave Bruno his biscuit.

'Now, Mary Ann, you go and hide behind the kitchen door,' continued Jack, chuckling to himself. 'When we want you, we'll send for you.'

Ronan waited for a minute, then twisted his body to get as much air into his chest as possible and said loudly, 'Bruno, find Mary Ann.'

Bruno shot out of the door and returned a moment later, towing the giggling Mary Ann along by her sleeve. Ronan laughed and laughed.

'Da?' he said to Mary Ann.

'Yes, when Da comes back we'll teach Bruno to find him, too,' said Mary Ann.

'He'll be back in five minutes or so, Ronan,' said Jack. 'We'll leave Bruno here with you; if you want anything, send him for me or Mary Ann.'

'He'll be your waiter,' said Mary Ann merrily. 'You can pretend he's your servant and send him on messages.'

'Yes,' said Ronan happily. This was what he had always wanted. He loved organising people and sending them to do things for him. Now he had a big dog to do that for him.

'Stay with Ronan, Bruno,' said Jack, as he and Mary Ann left the room.

Bruno put his big head on the sofa next to Ronan's hand, and Ronan could feel the warm softness of his fur. He felt warm and safe and happy, lying there listening to the laughter from the gentlemen in the dining-room. He even thought he heard Daniel O'Connell's voice, shouting with laughter, above all the other voices.

And then came another sound, from the hallway outside. Ronan froze as he listened. The voice wasn't loud – only a hissing whisper – but the words were clear.

'Was that crippled boy there when we were talking?'

And then the other voice, a little louder, contemptuous. 'What does it matter? The boy is an idiot. He can't talk, anyway. His pretty little sister pretends to understand him, but it's obvious that she just makes something up.'

In the warm, dimly lit room, Ronan smiled to himself. *Good*, he thought contentedly. *If they think I can't understand, I might hear more of their plans.*

Chapter Seven

The minute Ronan woke up the next morning his active brain went to work on the problem of Daniel O'Connell. Immediately he began to plan his day.

'Quick,' he said to his father. 'Quick ... me up.'

Michael rolled over in the comfortable bed of straw that had been laid down for them in the stable, stretched, sneezed and then sat up. He squinted through the window at the sun.

'What's the hurry?' he said sleepily. 'It's still early. Listen, that's the courthouse clock striking seven.' Let's talk about going to France. Do you know, Ronan, if I make that cupboard for Jack Carmody, there might be another five or ten pounds to put into the going-to-France box.'

Ronan looked at his father impatiently. He didn't need to say anything. Michael could read the question in his eyes.

'We'll probably need about another hundred pounds before we can go,' Michael said sadly, then he added cheerfully, 'Never mind, we'll get there in the end.'

Ronan lost interest in the conversation then. He hated waiting for things to happen.

'Me up,' he said again. He wanted to be out and waiting when Daniel O'Connell made his first appearance. He wanted to look at all the men who followed him about. Who was this Smith? And what disguise could he be wearing – a disguise so clever that no one would ever recognise him?

'Oh, all right,' said his father with a sigh. He knew it was no good arguing with Ronan. From the age of four or five, Ronan had commanded and organised the whole household. He always knew what needed to be done and who should do it. 'I'll just go and get some hot water, and then I'll wash and dress you. Someone's up, anyway; I see smoke coming from the kitchen chimney.'

The kitchen was full of people by the time Michael pushed Ronan, dressed in his best clothes again, into the room. Jack was there, with his wife Betsey, as fat, jolly, and kind as Jack himself. Mary Ann was there, giggling with one of the waitresses; she had spent the night in the maidservants' bedroom. And, best of all, Bruno was there. As soon as he saw Ronan, he came flying across the room. Ronan flinched, but then he twisted himself to gather all the air he could into his chest and said firmly and clearly, 'Bruno, find Mary Ann.'

Bruno spun around, huge tail wagging, shot across the room, grabbed the startled Mary Ann by the sleeve and dragged her over to Ronan's chair. Ronan laughed so much that his body went into a spasm and Michael had to hold him to stop him slipping through the leather straps. Ronan didn't mind. He loved this trick with the dog. *I'll teach him to find everyone and line them all up in front of me whenever I feel like it*, he thought.

'Hand,' he said to his father.

'He wants to pat the dog,' explained Mary Ann. Michael took one of Ronan's thin hands and moved it across the soft fur of the big dog's head. Bruno wagged his tail and licked Ronan's cheek.

'I'll give you your breakfast now, Ronan,' said Mary Ann, 'and then, after I've helped serve the gentlemen's breakfast, I'll take you around the town. It won't be as crowded as it was yesterday evening.'

'Ned,' jeered Ronan, but Mary Ann tossed her head and went over to get his breakfast without answering. Ronan smiled to himself. He had decided that he didn't like Ned at all, and he didn't think his father liked him either. He would have to get Mary Ann away from Ned, he thought, as he swallowed the spoonfuls of hot, sweet porridge. Ned might turn out like his father and spend all his time and money in pubs. *Mary Ann mustn't be allowed to marry him*, decided Ronan. *Da and I will find a nice husband for her*.

Still, he had more important things to plan first. He put them in order in his mind as he waited impatiently for Mary Ann to wipe his face with a clean rag.

'Cupboard,' he said to his father.

'Sorry?' said Michael.

'Cupboard,' said Ronan again. *You want to copy the cupboard in the dining-room. You need to look at it again.*

'Oh, yes, of course – the cupboard, the one you want me to make a copy of,' said Michael to Jack Carmody. 'Could I have another look at it? Would it be all right if I went into the dining-room?'

'Surely,' said Jack. 'There's none of them down yet, but even if there were, what harm?'

'Me,' said Ronan.

'I'll take Ronan, too,' said Michael. 'He has a great eye for detail. He has a great sense of what looks good, too. He sits with me in my workshop and gives me orders.'

'Bruno,' Ronan called as his father pushed him out of the room, and the big dog obediently followed them, his nose by Ronan's hand.

The dining-room was empty when they went in, but soon all of the gentlemen began to come in for their breakfast. The waitresses, with frilly caps and white frilly aprons over their long black dresses, came in as soon as the tables began to fill. Mary Ann was as good as any of them, Ronan thought. In fact, she seemed quicker than a lot of them, and she never stopped smiling. Ronan noticed another couple of sixpences being put into her hand. *That's at least three shillings and sixpence now*, he thought.

Daniel O'Connell seemed to be fine this morning, he thought, glancing over to where the big man sat in the corner of the room. He was in good spirits, as usual, and his table seemed to have the most shouts of laughter. He saw Ronan and Michael looking at the cupboard and gave them a cheery wave. He said something to John Steele about being slow at counting money, and John Steele laughed – he didn't seem to mind being teased. Daniel O'Connell looked across at Ronan and winked, and Ronan was able to wink back.

'Daniel O'Connell . . . clever,' he said to his father.

Michael nodded. 'He's the cleverest lawyer in the whole of Ireland, and England too, probably,' he whispered. Ronan nodded with satisfaction. He liked clever people; stupid people bored him. He was proud to be a spy for such a clever man.

As soon as breakfast was over, Mary Ann reappeared, ready to take Ronan out around the town. *She came very quickly*, thought Ronan. She hated washing-up; she had probably used him as an excuse not to help in the kitchen, and Jack and Betsey would be too softhearted to stop her going.

The streets of the town were still crowded, but not as crowded as they had been the day before. The sun was out, and it was already quite hot. Ronan loved the sun. When he was warm his back didn't ache as much as usual.

'Let's go down to the river,' said Mary Ann. 'Everyone will be down there.'

'Ned,' accused Ronan. *You just want to see Ned.*

'Did you see the money I got last night from the gentlemen at the tables?' said Mary Ann quickly. She knew Ronan well; he was always thinking up ways of making money.

Ronan looked a question.

'Five shillings and sixpence,' replied Mary Ann triumphantly.

'Box,' said Ronan instantly. *Put it in the going-to-France box.*

Mary Ann's face fell. She looked around at all the market stalls in the square, filled with all sorts of nice things to wear and to eat.

'Do you know, one of the gentlemen last night asked me what I wanted to do when I was grown up; and when I told him I want to be an actress, he said that a famous actress called Harriet Smithson was born here in Ennis and used to act in her father's theatre here when she was my age. She's twenty-eight now, and she acts in

Shakespeare plays in London. He said that I could be like her. Imagine it, Ronan – me acting in plays in London, and you sitting there watching me! We'd have loads of money then.'

'Box,' said Ronan sternly. He liked listening to Mary Ann's dreams of the future, but he preferred his father's dream of going to France and being in the sun. Mary Ann would spend the money on something silly if he didn't get a promise from her soon.

'Oh, all right,' said Mary Ann sadly. Then she cheered up. 'I'll just keep sixpence to buy some sweets and a few things for each of us.'

Giving Ronan no chance to say anything else, she pushed his chair into a corner and rapidly crossed the square. Ronan's mouth began to water. He had only tasted sweets once or twice in his life, but he loved them. There was that lovely taste trickling down his throat, and then afterwards a great feeling of energy and well-being.

'Are you crippled?' asked a hoarse voice beside him. Ronan turned his head and saw a very dirty small boy, holding a large pig by a piece of string tied around its hind leg.

'Good pig,' said Ronan, as clearly as he could. He ignored the remark about being crippled. He always ignored stupid remarks.

'He's fat, isn't he?' said the boy. 'I've been bringing him all around the streets of Ennis. I bring him to the back doors of the hotels, and they give us all the bits that the rich people leave on their plates. I eat some of it myself and give the rest to the pig. What's your name?'

'Ronan,' said Ronan. His own name was a word that he had difficulty in saying, so he was surprised when the boy repeated, 'Ronan.'

'You . . . name?' he asked.

Again, the boy replied readily. 'I'm Jimmy,' he said.

Ronan decided that Jimmy wasn't stupid after all. Together they watched the crowds of people milling around, greeting each other and beginning to line up by the booths in the hope that the voting would start soon.

'I'd give you a ride around the square if I didn't have the pig to hold,' said Jimmy in his hoarse voice. 'Bejapers, what's that? Is that a dog?'

Bruno was walking up Church Street. He bounded across the square and stopped at Ronan's chair, big tail wagging, big brown eyes full of love.

'Mine,' said Ronan proudly, and Jimmy's eyes widened with admiration. Ronan looked at the dog and wondered whether to tell him to find Mary Ann; but she had just reached the top of the queue at the sweet stall, so he decided to wait. He looked at Bruno thoughtfully. What could he get him to do?

Then an idea came to him. 'String,' he said to Jimmy. It was a difficult word for him to say, and he was just about to say it again when Jimmy produced a piece of string from his pocket. Ronan was delighted. His new friend was clever.

'Dog,' he said. This time Jimmy looked a little puzzled. Ronan made an effort. 'Dog . . .' he repeated. 'Like pig.'

'Oh, you want me to tie the string to the dog's collar,' said Jimmy. In a moment it was done.

'Chair,' said Ronan impatiently; and, obediently, Jimmy tied the other end of the string to the chair. Ronan made another great effort. He would have liked to order Jimmy to pull him up in the chair – he could speak so much better when he was sitting up straight – but Jimmy was so small and thin that he didn't look able to do it properly. He would just have to try and get the words out as well as possible, so that Bruno could understand him.

'Bruno, find Mary Ann,' he shouted.

The big dog set off immediately. He got a shock when he realised that Ronan's chair was rolling along behind him, but after a minute he got used to it. He walked slowly and carefully across the square, and everyone stood back to let them pass.

Mary Ann had just got her bag of sweets when they reached her. She giggled when she saw Ronan and the dog. She popped a sweet into Ronan's mouth and one into her own.

'Bruno,' ordered Ronan. Mary Ann held out a sweet on her palm and Bruno took it delicately, his enormous lips closing carefully over it.

'Boy,' Ronan said, so Mary Ann reluctantly dropped a sweet into Jimmy's filthy hand. She looked doubtfully at the pig, and then at her brother; but, luckily, Ronan had no immediate use for the pig, so he gave no further orders. Mary Ann quickly tucked the bag into her pocket.

'I'd better untie Bruno,' she said. 'Mr Carmody might be looking for him. I'll push you, and we'll go down to the river and see all the people.'

Chapter Eight

veryone was obeying the priests' order about not drinking, Ronan thought as they strolled along. The pubs seemed to be empty; the owners were standing disconsolately at the doors and even, in a few cases, offering a free drink to anyone who would come in. 'Sure, one drink won't break your pledge,' coaxed one of the innkeepers; but all the passers-by just shook their heads and turned their eyes away.

'There's Ned,' said Mary Ann eagerly. Ned was across the road, with his father.

'Who's Ned?' asked Jimmy.

'Stupid,' explained Ronan. *A stupid boy that Mary Ann likes.*

'No, he's not stupid,' said Mary Ann hotly. 'He's my friend. You can stay with your friend Jimmy and your friend the pig.' With that, she dashed after Ned.

'Is that his da?' asked Jimmy, looking at Thady.

'Stupid pig,' said Ronan with a friendly grin. He directed his eyes towards the pig, and then towards Thady, and Jimmy began to laugh. He laughed so much that the pig turned his head around and looked at him with surprise. This made Ronan laugh too, and the pair of them howled with laughter – until Ronan saw something that made him suddenly stop.

'No!' he said. 'Pub!'

'What's the matter?' asked Jimmy, wiping the sweat from Ronan's forehead with the edge of his dirty sleeve. He followed the direction of Ronan's eyes. 'Let him go into the pub. What do you care?'

Ronan stared in agony at the door of a little dark pub by the river. Thady had been welcomed in by the pub owner, and probably offered a free drink. He would get drunk – and everyone knew what happened when Thady Dooley got drunk: he immediately picked a fight with anyone who appeared. If a fight started, the streets of Ennis would be cleared, and none of the forty-shilling freeholders would be able to vote for Daniel O'Connell.

Ronan looked at Jimmy dubiously. Would he be able to make him understand?

'No pub,' he said. 'Father Murphy . . . no pub. You. . . . ' *You get him out of the pub!*

Jimmy shook his head. 'How could I get a fellow like that out of a pub?' he pleaded. 'Sure, he'd just swipe me across the head if I tried. Look, Ronan, I've got to go now. I have to bring the pig down to Carmody's Hotel. They'll be wanting to get rid of the breakfast leftovers. I'll be back in a while.'

With that, Jimmy tugged at the string around the pig's leg and pulled him back along the road towards Church Street. Ronan stared resentfully at the string tied to his chair. If only Mary Ann had left Bruno tied to his chair, the big dog could have pulled him along; he could have gone with his new friend Jimmy and visited all the back doors of the pubs and the hotels of Ennis. He directed an angry glance across the street at Mary Ann, who was looking down at the river with Ned. She offered him a sweet, and that made Ronan even angrier. The taste of his own sweet had gone from his mouth and left him wanting another one.

It seemed hours to Ronan before Mary Ann turned her head and saw him sitting there, alone and miserable. She ran over to him.

'Oh, Ronan, I'm sorry,' she said. 'I didn't know you were by yourself. I thought that boy and the pig were still with you.'

Quickly she popped a sweet in his mouth, and as Ronan sucked it he began to feel better. Ned was still over by the railings, looking at the river. He would get Mary Ann away from Ned, he decided.

'Back,' he said sternly. 'Back. Quick, quick.'

'Don't you want to come and look at the river?' coaxed Mary Ann. 'There's a swan family there with some baby swans. Would you like to see them? I'll get Ned to help me with the chair on the grass.'

'No,' said Ronan. 'Back.' He had a job to do. He planned to get hold of Father Murphy and send him into the pub after Thady. Jimmy was right: Thady wouldn't come out of the pub for a pig-boy. He wouldn't come out for Mary Ann, for Ronan, or even for Michael. There was only one man who might be able to get him out before it was too late, and that was Father Murphy. Everyone was a bit afraid of the priest, though they knew he was a good man.

'No,' said Mary Ann. 'I'm not going back. I'm having fun here. Some of Ned's friends are coming in a minute. Why should I spend my life looking after you?'

She looked away from him and her cheeks turned pink. For a minute Ronan felt a bit sorry for her, but then he was filled with fury. He never could bear not to get his own way.

'Stupid,' he said scathingly.

'And I'm fed up with you calling me stupid!' yelled Mary Ann. She seized the back of the chair and rattled him at breakneck speed over the rough cobbles of Mill

Street and past the courthouse in the square, to Carmody's Hotel.

'Stay there, then,' she said, parking his chair beside the entrance to the hotel and running away without a backward glance.

As time passed, Ronan began to be sorry that he had called Mary Ann stupid. He was bored stiff. He had seen Daniel O'Connell, but only for a few moments; and there had been no stranger with him, so there was no danger to warn him about. He was tired of watching the queues in front of the voting booths in the square, and there was no sign of Father Murphy anywhere – and, in any case, he doubted whether the priest would understand him without Mary Ann to interpret for him. He hadn't even seen Jimmy and the pig. *I suppose they're going around the back doors of all the hotels and inns,* he thought. *They won't come here, where all the rich gentlemen and ladies are walking. The rich people wouldn't like the pig under their feet.*

The courthouse clock struck eleven, and then twelve, and then one o'clock before anyone came – and then it was Michael, not Mary Ann.

'Oh, Ronan,' he said. 'You must be hungry. You poor boy! Where is that Mary Ann?'

'River, Ned,' said Ronan briefly. He did feel hungry, now that he thought about it. There were delicious smells coming from the dining-room of Carmody's Hotel.

'Dinner,' he added firmly. He didn't want his father to go off looking for Mary Ann now. She would get into trouble later – he was so angry with her for giving him such a boring morning that he wanted to get her into trouble – but he wanted to have his dinner first.

'Come into the kitchen,' said Michael, and wheeled him in.

Bruno gave Ronan a great welcome. He was careful not to jump up on Ronan any more, but he walked around and around the chair, his big tail wagging and his soft brown eyes full of love. Ronan swallowed the soup and then bits of a delicious meat pasty, and began to feel much better. He thought about getting his father to find Father Murphy, but he decided that it would be better to explain the matter through Mary Ann. She was the best at understanding him.

'Bruno, find Mary Ann,' he said, looking hopefully at the big dog.

Bruno circled around the room, looking puzzled, and then went to the door and barked. Betsey Carmody, on her way out, opened the door for him, and Bruno disappeared.

'That's too hard for him,' said Michael. 'Mary Ann could be anywhere in the town. How is he going to find her?'

Ronan didn't bother answering. He had great faith in Bruno. And he wanted Mary Ann. He felt odd without her. She was always with him. Ever since they had been babies, she had been his arms and his legs, and often his tongue. He couldn't do without her.

His father looked at him and seemed to understand what he was thinking.

'She's growing up fast, Ronan,' he said. He spoke quietly, almost as if he were talking to himself. 'She'll be off getting married in a few years' time. Still, you'll always have me, you know. Don't you worry. You and I will go into the furniture business, won't we? I'll make a big sign that says, "Michael McMahon & Son," and put it over the gate at Drumshee. What do you think about that?'

Ronan nodded, but he wasn't as interested as usual in his father's dreams. He was straining his ears to hear the sound of Bruno's claws clicking on the wooden passageway that led from the back door to the kitchen. Maybe it was too difficult for Bruno to find Mary Ann. Maybe there were too many people, too many streets, in Ennis. It wouldn't be like trying to find someone on the twenty acres of Drumshee.

'Door,' he ordered, and his father wheeled him over to the door from the kitchen. Still there was no sign of Bruno.

I'll count up to three hundred in my mind, Ronan decided. That would be five minutes, he worked out. It would take Bruno about that long to drag Mary Ann back from the river – but it might take him about five minutes to find her. *Better make it six hundred*, he decided. He began going through the numbers in his mind, his eyes intent and serious.

Michael sat at the kitchen table, watched his son's face and sighed. It would have been different if the twins' mother had lived, he thought for the millionth time. She would have helped him to care for their disabled son and taken some of the burden off Mary Ann's shoulders. Ronan was so disabled and also so strong-willed that the household revolved around him, and Mary Ann's needs got pushed to the background. It wasn't easy for her, Michael thought. Perhaps that was why she took refuge in acting out little plays all the time. He decided that he wouldn't be cross with her when she came back. She deserved a little fun sometimes.

'Ronan,' he said gently. 'You know Mary Ann does a lot for you. You must try to be nice to her, now. Don't always expect her to be with you. She has her own life to lead. You mustn't be selfish.'

Ronan felt quite shocked. For a moment he lost track of the numbers passing through his head. His gentle father had never criticised him before. Was he selfish? He tried to put the idea to the back of his mind, but he knew his father was right.

I won't say anything to her, he thought. *I'll just manage the job of looking after Daniel O'Connell all by myself.* He gave a nod to show his father that he understood, and then went back to listening for Mary Ann's return. It must be at least six hundred seconds since Bruno had left. *Six hundred and one*, he thought, *six hundred and two* . . . .

'You can stay with me this afternoon, Ronan, don't worry,' Michael said aloud; but Ronan ignored him. He was listening intently for any sound outside, though his mind still visualised the numbers passing along in a long line. Six hundred and fifty-seven! Surely Bruno had found Mary Ann by now. Six hundred and sixty. . . . And then, suddenly, a whisper from a room down the passageway interrupted his concentration. He recognised it; he had heard that voice whisper before.

'They say the boy isn't an idiot,' came the whisper. 'They say he can count and add up.'

'Don't worry,' came the reply. 'I told you – the sister just makes it up. She's a clever little thing.'

'Yes, but what if –'

'Well, if there's a problem, Smith will deal with it. One push, and the boy's chair would be in the river. There would be nothing he could do.'

Then there was a low chuckle. Ronan felt his heart start to thump and his hands grow sweaty. He looked over at his father, but Michael didn't seem to have heard, and there was no one else in the kitchen. Again he decided that this would be too difficult for him to explain to his father.

He began to count again. Seven hundred, seven hundred and one, seven hundred and two. . . . And then, at last, there was an excited bark and there was Bruno, and with him Mary Ann. She was looking embarrassed and ashamed; both Ronan and Michael noticed. She wheeled Ronan's chair back into the kitchen, avoiding their eyes.

'Come and have something to eat,' said Michael gently. Ronan stared resolutely at the fire, ignoring his sister. Inwardly, though, he was chuckling. He knew Mary Ann would do anything he wanted for the afternoon. Things were working out very well. Again the memory of the men's whispered words flitted across his mind, but he pushed them away. Mary Ann would stay with him from now on, and he would be safe from them.

He smiled at Bruno, who was looking anxiously into his face. *If only I had Bruno with me all the time*, he thought. He could have the whole household summoned whenever he wanted them. Bruno would be able to bite those men – would be able to kill this Smith, whoever he was.

He was still smiling at Bruno when Mary Ann came over, a meat pasty in one hand, and ruffled his hair with her free hand.

'Where would you like to go this afternoon, Ro-Ro?' she asked. 'Ro-Ro' had been her name for him when they were little, and she still used it whenever she was feeling especially fond of him.

'River,' he said promptly.

She looked at him with surprise. 'But –' she started to say, but he interrupted her.

'Thady,' he said. *Thady went into the pub. If he's still there, he'll be drunk when he comes out; he'll start a fight, and then the soldiers will send everyone home and Daniel O'Connell won't be elected.* He stared at her intently, willing her to understand.

'Oh, yes,' said Mary Ann with a guilty flush. Ronan relaxed. She knew what he meant. 'I'll be back at half past four, Mrs Carmody,' she said to Betsey Carmody, who had just come back into the kitchen. 'I'll be able to help with the cooking then, and I'll have plenty of time to get changed before serving dinner.'

'You enjoy yourself, dear,' said Mrs Carmody placidly.

'I'll meet you in the square at half past four,' said Michael. 'Make sure that you leave Ronan with me, or take him into the hotel. I don't like him being left alone in the streets.'

'Yes, Da,' murmured Mary Ann, looking embarrassed again and taking another bite from her meat pasty. Ronan stared at her.

'Bruno, meat,' he ordered, and Mary Ann meekly gave Bruno the last bit of her pasty before they went out.

Thady wasn't the only one who had gone to the riverside pub, Ronan realised as they drew near it. The sound of at least two voices, singing raucously, came from the small tumbledown building.

'Ned,' said Ronan, his quick eye noticing the tall figure of Ned lounging beside the river.

'Oh, Ned, could you get your da out of the pub?' pleaded Mary Ann.

'No, I couldn't,' said Ned firmly. 'He wouldn't come out for me.'

'You,' said Ronan to Mary Ann. He remembered how she had put the wild rose in Thady's buttonhole outside the church at Corofin. He looked around. Yes, there were some wild orchids growing on the riverbank.

'Flowers,' he said. The word wasn't very clear, but Mary Ann followed the direction of his eyes and understood. For a moment she looked as if she was going to refuse; but then she obviously remembered how she had left him to himself for the whole morning. She went over to the riverbank and picked a few flowers. Ronan could see by her eyes that she was thinking about what to say to Thady. It would be like a little play for her, he knew. He started to grin.

Mary Ann smoothed her curls and then went over to the door of the pub.

'Mr Dooley, Mr Dooley,' she called in a high, childish voice. 'Mr Dooley, I've got something for you.'

'Tha'sh tha' sweet little girl of Mich'l McMa'n,' said Thady Dooley's voice. 'She's a li'l dote. Come on, Barty, come an' see her.'

Obviously Thady wasn't yet fighting drunk, Ronan thought as Thady staggered to the doorway, his arm around another man. Both of them were smiling foolishly.

'Look, Mr Dooley,' continued Mary Ann, smiling prettily and holding out the flowers to him, but taking a step backwards.

'Flowers for me, dotey? You love ol' Thady, don't you? Give us a kiss.'

Mary Ann took another step backwards, still holding out the flowers. Ronan thought rapidly. It would be no good; Thady would just turn around and go back into the pub as soon as he was given the flowers, or the kiss.

'River,' he said quickly. Seeing Mary Ann hesitate, he hissed, 'River, like Da, Uncle John.' *Remember how Da knocked Uncle John into the river when he got drunk?* John had had a row with Nora; he had gone to the pub for hours and come home fighting drunk, and Michael had knocked him into the river. John had turned sober in an instant, seen Mary Ann and Ronan laughing, and started to laugh himself. Mary Ann and Ronan had teased him about it for months afterwards. The only problem was that Mary Ann wasn't big and strong enough to knock Thady into the river. He saw her look across at Ned, but Ned avoided her eyes and turned his back.

Mary Ann looked back at Thady and smiled invitingly. 'Oh, if you want a kiss, you'll have to come and get it, Mr Dooley,' she said saucily.

She did it very cleverly, Ronan decided. Every time Thady got within kissing distance of her, she took another step backwards, waving her bunch of flowers. Step by step she moved across the grass, and step by step she got nearer and nearer to the river. Thady followed her, still with his arm around the shoulders of his drinking companion. *I hope she knows how near she is*, thought Ronan; a*nother step and she'll be in the river herself.*

'Which do you want, Mr Dooley – the kiss or the flowers?' cried Mary Ann. She leaned forward, stuck the bunch of flowers right under his nose, and stepped neatly to one side just as he leaned forwards.

There was a tremendous splash and a roar of anger, cut off rapidly by a gurgling sound. Ronan wished he were a bit nearer the riverbank, so that he could see right down into the water, but he could guess what was going on by the sounds. Obviously the other man, the man called Barty, wasn't quite as drunk as Thady. Ronan could hear him shouting Thady's name. After a minute, two figures climbed up the muddy bank and stood there, swaying, with water pouring down their faces and dripping from their clothes.

Ronan burst out laughing. He saw Ned looking at him crossly, but he couldn't stop. Little crowing sounds came from him, and his legs twitched with amusement.

'Oh, Mr Dooley,' said Mary Ann, standing her ground bravely. 'Oh, you poor, poor man, look how wet you are! Oh, poor Mr Dooley!'

Thady looked at her. He was almost sober again, Ronan thought; his eyes were much clearer. He stared at Mary Ann, but she kept the sweet, anxious smile fixed on her face.

Thady turned on Ned. 'You ignorant scoundrel!' he yelled. 'You're the one that tripped me and knocked me into the water – and you didn't even have the decency to pull me out again. I'll give you a beating you won't forget!'

He threw himself on Ned, knocking him to the ground, kicking him, and thumping him with his fists. Ronan wasn't particularly sorry for Ned, but he was worried that a policeman might come along and think it was a fight. Luckily, the man called Barty grabbed Thady by the arm and dragged him off Ned.

'Come on, Thady,' he said. 'My house is just around the corner. I'll give you some dry clothes. Come on. Leave the boy alone.'

Ronan watched the two of them go. He had a smile on his face. That had worked beautifully.

Ned was struggling to his feet. One of his eyes was already beginning to swell up, and he was rubbing his leg where his father had kicked him.

'That's your fault,' he hissed at Mary Ann. 'You're responsible for that, you stupid vixen. You and that idiot brother of yours.'

'Don't you call my brother an idiot!' yelled Mary Ann, flinging the bunch of flowers in his face. 'I'm never going to speak to you again, Ned Dooley. Just you keep away from me.'

'Don't worry,' said Ned bitterly, limping away. 'I never want to see you again for the rest of my life. I'll pay you back – and I'll pay back that cripple. I saw him laughing at me.'

Chapter Nine

Ronan and Mary Ann had a great time that afternoon. Mary Ann didn't seem to miss Ned at all, Ronan noticed. Probably she had got tired of hanging around with him. Ned was stupid, just like his stupid father, and Mary Ann was used to being with clever people like her own father and brother.

At the end of the afternoon, everyone gathered outside the courthouse to hear the result of the election.

'We need a re-count,' announced the Returning Officer. An angry sound rose from the crowd, but he ignored it, turned on his heel and went rapidly back into the courthouse.

'We'll have to stay another night, Ronan,' whispered Mary Ann.

'What are they trying to do?' asked Michael McMahon despairingly. 'Everyone knows that Daniel O'Connell has twice as many votes as Vesey Fitzgerald.'

Ronan felt sorry that it was disappointing for Daniel O'Connell, but he was thrilled to stay another night in Ennis. He knew that Mary Ann felt the same.

'Stay with me, my friends,' shouted Daniel O'Connell. 'Together we'll win this election and we'll win Catholic Emancipation. They can't hold back the tide now.'

And so everyone stayed, and Ronan sat in the hotel parlour bar for the whole evening and watched Daniel O'Connell every minute. No strange man came near the Liberator, and no word of the man Smith was spoken in Ronan's hearing.

The next morning, Mary Ann was still in a very repentant mood.

'If you'll wait five minutes while I change my dress, Ronan,' she said, 'then you can choose everything that we do today.' She bent down and whispered, 'And I'll buy some more sweets.'

'Out,' said Ronan peremptorily. 'Daniel O'Connell.' *I want to keep an eye on Daniel O'Connell.*

'Oh, all right,' said Mary Ann. 'You wait outside the hotel, in the sun. You can keep an eye on all the men outside, and I'll be out in five or ten minutes.'

So Ronan sat outside, with the sun warming his bones and making him feel so comfortable that, for the thousandth time, he imagined what it would be like to live in France – to have hot sun shining on him for the whole summer, the way his aunt Caitriona described in her letters. Daniel O'Connell still looked happy and confident this morning, thought Ronan, watching the great man stroll up Church Street with his friends and disappear into the courthouse. Perhaps today would be the day he would be elected as Member of Parliament. . . .

But if that happened, Ronan suddenly remembered, that would be the moment of greatest danger. That was when the disguised Smith would stick a knife in Daniel O'Connell's ribs and then disappear through the crowd. *It's my job to find Smith before he can kill Daniel O'Connell*, he thought, turning his face towards the sun.

And then, suddenly, the light of the sun was blotted out. Ronan's nostrils were filled with the stench of wool. Someone had thrown something over his head – it was the shawl that Mary Ann had wrapped around his knees. He screamed, but the scream was cut off before it left his mouth; a strong hand forced a wodge of the strong-smelling wool into his mouth. And then his chair was seized from behind and rattled along over the cobblestones, going down the slope of the road at breakneck speed.

No one who is as disabled and helpless as Ronan can ever live without knowing fear. Ronan had often been frightened. He had been frightened whenever he woke from a nightmare and his father wasn't there. He had been very frightened when he had been left alone in the kitchen and a burning piece of turf had fallen out of the fire and blazed up just beside the rag rug. He had been terrified the day that the bull had broken loose and charged across the yard towards where he was sitting. But he had never known such panic as overwhelmed him that day, when someone unknown seized his wheelchair and ran away with him.

It's Smith, he thought. *He's going to throw my chair in the river. We're going down Church Street towards the river.* He tried to imagine what it would be like to drown. He remembered a day when John had shouted from the yard, and Michael had turned his head towards the window and allowed Ronan to slip down in the bath. It had only been for a second, but Ronan still remembered the water over his mouth and nose, the terrible choking feeling – the feeling that his lifelong struggle to breathe had suddenly ended. The river would be worse than that, he thought. His vivid imagination made it so real to him that he felt a violent spasm almost tear his chest apart. He had slumped down in his chair; the woollen cloth was blocking his mouth; it was always hard for him to cough properly, but now it was almost impossible. His whole body was racked with spasms.

The chair rattled and bumped over the cobblestones. Whoever was pushing him was young and strong, he thought; someone with long legs, someone with heavy hobnailed boots – and some nails missing from the left boot, he noticed, even in the middle of his terror. And then another sound drove the footsteps from his mind. It was a splash – not a loud splash, probably just a duck flying in and landing with a noisy plop on the surface of the river, but it was enough to tell Ronan where they were. They were right beside the river.

The chair slowed down. They were off the cobbles and onto the grass of the riverbank. Ronan knew that the end was near. The whispered words that he had overheard were ringing in his head. '*One push and his chair will be in the river. . . .*' That was what the man in the hotel had whispered.

A deadly sick faintness came over him. If only he could scream! There were people around; he could hear voices, shouts of laughter. Why did no one notice him? He fought and struggled, trying desperately to spit the bad-tasting material out of his mouth.

Suddenly the chair stopped, with such a jerk that Ronan's head flopped forward onto his chest like the head of a strangled hen. He gagged. He was going to get sick, and he had no one to hold him; no one to make sure that the vomit did not go back into his lungs and choke him to death.

A muttered curse from behind him suddenly caught his attention. *I know that voice!* he thought. *Is it Smith's voice? Do I know Smith?* The surprise was so great that he stopped feeling sick. He deliberately allowed his legs to go into a violent spasm. Somebody might notice.

The chair was stuck, he realised. It had stuck in the soft mud next to the river. His enemy was trying to drag it backwards. Ronan's head flopped back. He was bumped and bruised, but he could breathe better now.

The woollen material had worked a little loose in his mouth.

Then he heard a voice just next to him, a shaky old voice, high-pitched and querulous. 'What are you doing with that little fellow? Take that shawl off his face!'

And in an instant the shawl was plucked from his face; he could breathe again. His cramped lungs sucked in great chestfuls of air. The sweat ran down his face. Wide with terror, his eyes saw nothing for a moment; then he realised that an old woman was standing in front of him, one filthy hand patting his cheek and the shawl dangling from the other.

'You poor little boy,' she crooned. 'That bad fellow's run away. He was playing a trick on you, wasn't he? You come home with old Madge. She'll look after you.'

Too late, Ronan thought of turning his head. There was no one behind him, but he could hear the heavy sound of hobnailed boots running back up Church Street.

'Who?' He struggled to make the old woman understand, but she took no notice.

'Yes, you come home with old Madge. She'll give you some nice cabbage soup. Wait a bit, though – here come the soldiers. Look, they're coming across the bridge. We'll wait until they've passed, lovey, and then I'll take you home.'

Stupid, thought Ronan. His panic was beginning to subside; the wild, painful thumping of his heart was slowing to a heavy beat, and the sweat on his face was drying in the hot sun. He sucked in another great lungful of air and waited for the spasms to pass away. He would feel better soon. He had learned that the terrible jerking passed more quickly if he said nothing and just tried to relax quietly.

He watched the soldiers with interest. He admired their red uniforms, the shine on their swords and their belt-buckles. All of their faces were very brown. Many of them had scars, though, like white seams across the brown skin. One of them had a scar all the way down his face; Ronan imagined the sword that had slashed him. Another had a puckered wound across his hand, and there was one with a scar over his eyebrow. It gave his face a funny look, thought Ronan. The soldier had very bright blue eyes, but the eye with the scar over it looked bigger and rounder than the other eye; the scar pulled up the eyebrow and gave him a look of surprise.

Ronan gave a small chuckle. He was beginning to feel better. Once the soldiers had passed, he would make the old woman take him back to Carmody's Hotel, and then Mary Ann would come find him and they would go around Ennis. Maybe they would take Bruno, too. Bruno would look after him, and the three of them would have a lovely day together.

'We go now,' he said to the old woman, as the last of the soldiers passed them.

'You be old Madge's baby,' crooned the old woman, kissing him on the cheek. *Stupid*, thought Ronan. He didn't care too much, though. He would soon be back at Carmody's Hotel.

The old woman moved away from him and muttered to a man who was walking briskly across the bridge. What was she saying? Ronan strained his ears. She was asking the man to lift the chair out of the mud. Maybe she wasn't so stupid, after all. Ronan didn't know the man, but he thought he had seen him before – a man from Kilrush, probably.

'You should keep that chair on the pavement, missus,' the man was saying. 'Here, Mick,' he shouted across the street, 'give us a hand with this, will you?'

The two men lifted the chair out of the soft, muddy ruts near the river and placed it on the pavement by the bridge.

'There you are, then,' said the first man.

'He's old Madge's baby,' muttered the old woman. She seized the back of Ronan's chair and began to push it. Ronan gave a startled shout. Old Madge was pushing his chair away from Church Street, towards the bridge.

'No – no!' he yelled. 'Back, back.'

'That's right, lovey,' mumbled the old woman. 'You're old Madge's baby, and she's going to take you home and put you by the fire, and you can have some nice cabbage soup.'

'No, no, stupid,' yelled Ronan. He was still slumped in his chair and he couldn't get many words out. Anyway, he guessed that old Madge was wandering in her mind.

Second childhood, his father called it. There were a few old people like that near Drumshee. Their children and grandchildren looked after them, and everyone politely agreed with whatever they said, no matter how stupid it sounded.

'They live in a world of their own, old people like that,' Michael had told Mary Ann, when she was trying to explain to one old woman that her cloth doll wasn't really a baby. 'Sure, they're happy there. Don't be bothering them by trying to explain things.'

I'll wait until we pass someone, thought Ronan. *I'll save my energy until I meet someone who isn't so stupid.*

So he sat in his wheelchair, tense and white-faced, as old Madge wheeled him across the bridge. They met no one; this part of town seemed almost deserted since the soldiers had passed. He had a moment's hope when the old woman paused outside a vegetable shop on the quay. She picked up a couple of cabbages and squeezed them, and the shopkeeper came out and glared suspiciously at her.

'Me . . . back . . . hotel,' Ronan said to the shop-keeper, but the man just stared at him in a puzzled, embarrassed way.

'Yes, yes,' said old Madge soothingly, popping several cabbages into her bag, but not attempting to pay for them. 'My baby wants some cabbage soup. Come on, then, little fellow.' Seizing the back of Ronan's chair, she pushed him on along the pavement. Almost before he knew what was happening, she had opened the door of a cabin-like little house and pushed his chair into a dark, smelly kitchen.

Chapter Ten

Muttering to herself, old Madge pulled the heads of cabbage out of her bag. It was no wonder the shopkeeper hadn't bothered chasing them, thought Ronan; most of the cabbage heads were pale yellow and had that disgusting smell that cabbage has when it is beginning to rot. In fact, he realised as his eyes got accustomed to the darkness inside the little house, the room was already full of half-rotten cabbages. That was why it smelt so bad. Cabbages were piled up on the rickety old table, heaped in a corner, stuffed into the bottom of the dresser and dumped on the sill of the one small window as breeding-places for flies.

Worst of all, though, was the smell from the cooking cabbage. *That must be the cabbage soup she kept talking about*, thought Ronan with dismay. He glanced quickly around the dark, smelly room, hoping desperately that this mad old woman had someone else living with her, someone who would take him back to his father. But there was no one there. He would have to make her understand.

'Me out,' he said loudly and harshly.

'Yes, my baby wants cabbage soup,' muttered old Madge. 'My baby wants to sit by the fire and have his cabbage soup.'

She put the latest cabbages on top of the others on the table. This made some of the older ones fall off onto the floor, but she didn't seem to notice. She wheeled Ronan's chair towards the fire; then she bent down and picked up a dirty plate and spoon off the floor, gave them a wipe with her filthy shawl, then ladled some soup into the plate.

'No!' shouted Ronan, but she took no notice. The dripping spoon held in her shaky old hand came nearer and nearer to his mouth. He turned his face away, thanking heaven that he could at least control his head.

'No,' he screamed again. 'No! No soup!'

'Yes, yes, you're a hungry baby,' muttered the old woman.

'No!' Ronan shouted. His legs began to jerk; he felt himself slipping down in his chair. The soft leather straps that should have been around his waist were now around his chest. He felt as if he couldn't breathe. He clenched his teeth, determined that not one drop of that horrible cabbage soup was going to pass his lips.

A sudden gust of wind sent a draught down the chimney, and a cloud of turf-smoke blew out into the room. Ronan started to cough. He had had bad coughs before; he had always hated them, but then he had had his father to hold him, to rub his back, to carry him around in the fresh air until he felt better. Now he thought that his chest would be torn apart. His stomach heaved, and he felt his face burn with the struggle to breathe.

Something of his distress seemed to penetrate old Madge's senile mind. She dropped the spoon and the dish on the hob and stared at him.

'Baby wants air,' she muttered. To Ronan's enormous relief, she opened the door and pushed his chair out onto the pavement. Several well-dressed people were passing by, and they looked at him curiously as he drew in loud, wheezing gulps of air.

'Me . . . hotel,' he managed to say to one lady who was staring at him. For a moment she hesitated, and he hoped that she had understood, but then she looked embarrassed and crossed to the other side of the street. He didn't waste time watching her go. A priest was coming down the street. At first Ronan thought it was Father Murphy; his heart leaped with excitement and hope, and his breathing began to ease. But then he saw that it was Father Coffey, the only priest in County Clare who was not supporting Daniel O'Connell. Still, it might be worth appealing to him.

'Father Murphy. . . .' *Father Murphy knows me. Take me to him.* He stared intently at the priest, willing him to understand; but, even to himself, the words hadn't sounded right. He didn't have enough breath to make any sound properly.

'Good boy, good boy,' murmured the priest mechanically. To Ronan's horror, he too began to cross the street.

'That's my baby, Father,' said old Madge, appearing out of the smoke-filled hovel. The priest made the sign of the cross in their direction and hurried on. Ronan could feel tears running down his cheeks. He closed his eyes in despair.

Then he opened them with a snap. He smelled something. It wasn't the smell of smoke, or the disgusting smell of rotting cabbages, or the even more disgusting smell of cabbage soup. This smell was more welcome to him than the scent of the lilac tree outside Drumshee on a May evening. It was the rich and unmistakeable smell of a well-fed pig. And then he heard Jimmy's hoarse voice shouting, 'Ronan!'

'Your da is looking for you everywhere,' said Jimmy, seizing the back of the chair. 'And your sister, too. She's crying like anything. How did you get down here? Now, how am I going to get you and the pig back up to Church Street?'

'No, no, that's my baby!' yelled old Madge, clutching at the side of the chair.

'Me back,' shouted Ronan to Jimmy.

Jimmy tried to push the chair; the old woman tugged it back towards the house; the pig squealed; Ronan shouted orders; the old woman screamed at Jimmy and started to beat him around the head with her broomstick. Jimmy let go of the chair to protect his head, and old Madge triumphantly pushed Ronan back into the smoke-filled, filthy house.

For most people it would have been all over, but Ronan did not give up easily. Even in the noise and confusion of the last few minutes, he had noticed the pig's greedy little eyes fixed longingly on the cabbages inside the house.

'Let go pig string!' he yelled. It was one of the loudest and clearest sentences he had ever uttered in his life. It wasn't a request, it was an order, and Jimmy reacted automatically: he dropped the string tied around the pig's leg. The pig plunged into the old woman's house and began devouring the cabbages as if he hadn't eaten for a month. Jimmy looked from the gobbling pig to the screaming woman trying to whack him with her broomstick – and decided that the safest thing to do was grab Ronan and run.

They rattled up the street at such a pace that Ronan thought he would be bounced out of his chair at any moment. Behind them ran the pig, still chewing on a large cabbage, and behind the pig came the old woman, whacking at it with her broomstick. Ronan glanced over his shoulder. Madge could run quite fast for such an old woman, he thought apprehensively. Soon she would catch up with them – and what would Jimmy do then? Would he let go of Ronan's chair and run away? After all, he was only about eight years old, and he was nervous of grown-up people. Old Madge was now within a few feet of them.

And then, suddenly, like an angel from heaven, a tall figure came running across the bridge. It was Ned, and Ronan had never been so glad to see him in his life.

'Be off home with you,' Ned shouted at the old woman.

She hesitated, but Ned was a big fellow. Finally she turned and went off, grumbling to herself.

'Grab the pig,' Ned added to Jimmy, putting his large boot on the string that dangled from the pig's hind leg.

Jimmy bent down and seized the string firmly, and Ned lifted his boot. Ronan stared at the print it had left in the mud beside the river. The mud was very soft, and the boot had left a clear print; he could see the pattern of the hobnails. And three of them were missing.

So it wasn't Smith; it was Ned who pushed me down the street and left me by the river, thought Ronan. A great flood of relief swept over him. He understood what had happened. Ned had been furious with Mary Ann and furious with Ronan; he had tried to revenge himself on them both by pushing Ronan away from outside the hotel. Ronan didn't care. He wasn't afraid of Ned; he knew Ned would never have had the nerve to drown him . . . unless Smith had told him to. Could he have done such a thing?

Ronan decided to try to forget about it all. He still had a job to do. Daniel O'Connell had been without his protection for the whole morning.

'Back,' he said severely, eyeing Ned coldly. 'Mary Ann,' he added meaningfully. *I'll tell Mary Ann what you've done.*

Ned's sunburnt face turned a deep red, but he gripped the back of the chair and trudged back up the hill, with Jimmy and the pig walking beside them. Ronan listened carefully: yes, he could hear the slightly uneven sound from the left boot. It was definitely Ned who had kidnapped him.

As soon as they came in sight of the hotel, Ned stopped abruptly. Mary Ann was standing outside the door. Betsey Carmody had an arm around her, and even from a distance they could hear Mary Ann's sobs.

'Here,' said Ned roughly to Jimmy, 'you push him.' Then he was gone; they could hear the uneven tread of his boots clattering back down Church Street.

'Stupid,' said Ronan with satisfaction.

'He could have gone the rest of the way,' grumbled Jimmy, looking at the pig and at Ronan. 'I'll never manage to push you and stop that pig getting away. Oh, there's your da,' he added with relief.

A minute later Ronan was being lifted out of his chair and into his father's arms, his chest supported by Michael's strong shoulder. It was wonderful to be able to breathe easily again.

'Old Madge had him,' explained Jimmy in his hoarse voice. 'She's a crazy old woman that lives down by the river.'

'So that's what Bruno was doing,' exclaimed Jack Carmody, stepping forward from the hotel porch, holding a heavily panting Bruno on a strong chain. 'He led me down to the river a dozen times. I was afraid. . . .' He broke off, but Ronan finished the sentence in his mind: *I was afraid that someone had pushed him in the river.* He smiled down at Bruno. Bruno had done his best; it was Jack who was too stupid to believe his clever dog. Poor old Bruno! Ronan knew how annoying it was when no one understood what you were trying to tell them.

'You're a great lad to have found him,' said Michael to Jimmy, and his voice was hoarse, too, with emotion. 'Here's a threepenny bit for you. Now let's get you inside, Ronan. Stop crying, Mary Ann. All's well that ends well!'

Once Ronan was in his father's arms, he almost felt like crying – crying out all the terror of the last few hours. It was so lovely to be back with his family, sitting with his father in the warm, clean kitchen of the hotel;

to have Mary Ann kneeling by his chair, rubbing warmth back into his thin cold hands, and the satisfying bulk of Bruno panting beside him. But he had something to do first. He took a deep breath and looked Mary Ann firmly in the eye.

'Ned . . . bad,' he said as clearly as he could. He saw her face pale and her eyes darken with anger, and knew that she understood him.

'What do you mean, Ronan?' asked Michael, puzzled, smiling his thanks to Betsey Carmody as she put a mug of warm milk into his hands. But Ronan said no more. It was enough that Mary Ann understood him. She would have nothing more to do with Ned. He and Mary Ann would be a pair again, and he would be able to concentrate on keeping Daniel O'Connell safe.

'Put the lad for a sleep on the couch in the reading-room,' said Jack Carmody, patting Ronan compassionately with his big red hand. 'He looks dead tired.'

'No!' cried Ronan. He still wasn't quite certain whether Smith had been involved in Ned's malice. He didn't want to be left alone ever again.

'Don't worry,' said Michael. 'I'll stay with you, Ronan. You've plenty of time for a sleep; it's only three o'clock. There's nothing more to be done now,' he added to Jack. 'They won't declare the results until about seven or eight this evening, but they're bound to declare Daniel O'Connell elected. Every vote has been counted twenty times over.'

Ronan relaxed in his father's arms and allowed himself to be placed on the leather couch. A warm, comforting rug was tucked around him. It was only as his eyelids were closing heavily over his eyes that a thought came to him. Tonight was the night when Daniel O'Connell would be in great danger – and Ronan still didn't know who this man Smith was and what disguise he would be wearing.

Chapter Eleven

It was a wonderful evening. Nobody minded waiting. By seven o'clock, the word had gone around that Daniel O'Connell had won by more than three votes for every one that Vesey Fitzgerald had managed to secure. Banners waved, bands boomed, tin whistles tooted, people danced and sang in the square.

Not everyone was happy, though. Vesey Fitzgerald and his men clustered in a little group, whispering to each other; several landlords, their faces dark with anger, stood silently waiting; the police and the army examined their guns and their truncheons.

And Ronan McMahon, the secret spy from Drumshee, sat tense and white-faced, his eyes fixed on Daniel O'Connell. Beside him were Jimmy – with his pig, of course – and Mary Ann, dancing a jig to the time of her tin whistle. But Ronan ignored them and the entire happy crowd around them. All his attention was concentrated on Daniel O'Connell.

Daniel O'Connell looked very happy too, Ronan thought. He stood on the steps of the courthouse, surrounded by plants and branches of greenery, and he looked as if he were king of the world. He would be the first Irish Catholic elected to the British Parliament, and then he would bring freedom and justice to the Catholics of Ireland. Catholics would be able to buy land, to become judges and doctors, to go to university and to have their own schools for their children. His friends were with him – there was John Steele, Gorman McMahon, several priests: Father Murphy was there, of course, and the priest from Kilrush, and Father. . . . But who was that priest standing behind Daniel O'Connell?

Ronan's attention suddenly sharpened. It was strange that he hadn't noticed this priest before; he had thought he knew all the priests around Daniel O'Connell by now. And this priest was an unusual-looking man: he had very bright blue eyes, but one of them had a scar over it and looked bigger and rounder than the other eye. The scar pulled up the man's eyebrow, giving him a look of surprise. *I know that face, though*, thought Ronan.

Suddenly Ronan knew where he had seen the priest before. He hadn't been dressed as a priest then, though. He had been one of the soldiers who had marched across the bridge that morning, when Ronan had been with old Madge. What was a soldier doing dressed as a priest, standing behind Daniel O'Connell?

In less time than it takes to draw breath, Ronan had the answer. This was Smith — Smith in a disguise that meant no one would suspect him. And he was there to slip a knife into Daniel O'Connell the instant that the result was announced. Then he would disappear — probably pretending to get a doctor or something, thought Ronan. No one would suspect a priest.

Ronan narrowed his eyes. The last rays of the setting sun shone on the little group on the courthouse steps. The false priest moved his right hand quickly to the sleeve of his left, but his movement wasn't quite quick enough: Ronan caught a glimpse of something silver glinting just below the left cuff. It was Smith. And he had a knife.

What was there to do? Ronan looked at Bruno. He could send Bruno to drag Daniel O'Connell away, but it mightn't work. Ronan knew that all the people Bruno had dragged to him had been willing to come and had been joining in a game. The Returning Officer had just appeared at the door of the courthouse. Every face was turned towards him. Daniel O'Connell would not be willing to move at this, the greatest moment of his life.

Suddenly Ronan's brain snapped into action. He had noticed, earlier, that Jimmy's pig had been looking at the greenery on the courthouse steps with the same longing look he had had in his greedy little eyes when he had seen the cabbages in old Madge's house. The same trick might work again.

There was not a moment to be lost. Ronan opened his mouth, sucked in a great lungful of air and yelled, 'Let . . . go . . . string!'

And Jimmy automatically dropped the string. The pig plunged forward, cleaving his way through the crowd like a scythe through the hay on Drumshee meadows. The crowd of people fell back, laughing, but getting out of his way as fast as possible – everyone knew what it was like to be trampled by a hungry pig. In the middle of all the noise and confusion, Ronan took another gulp of air.

'Look! Priest . . . scar . . . knife . . . kill . . . Daniel O'Connell!' he shouted at Mary Ann; and, miraculously, she understood him. Like Ronan's, her mind worked fast – and, unlike Ronan's, her feet were fast too. Without a second's hesitation, she followed the pig through the crowd, screaming loudly and dramatically.

Those who saw Mary Ann act when she was grown up often argued over which was the best part she had ever played. What they never knew was that the best piece of acting Mary Ann had ever done was when she was twelve years old and had two minutes in which to save Daniel O'Connell's life.

She was magnificent. She shrieked, she screamed, she wailed; she made such a noise that even the bands stopped playing. Everyone was looking at her. She darted here and there, pretending to make elaborate and dramatic efforts to catch the pig, but all the time driving him nearer and nearer to the courthouse steps.

'Stop him! Stop him!' she cried, and the crowd roared with laughter. This was as good as a play!

For a moment Ronan felt a stab of fear. Would Smith grab the opportunity, amid all the chaos, to plunge his knife into Daniel O'Connell?

Fortunately, however, Daniel O'Connell was enjoying the fun as much as the crowd in the square. He crossed over to the other side of the steps, moving in front of John Steele, in order to see the scene better. He threw back his great head and roared with laughter. 'Come on, Mary Ann,' he shouted. 'You nearly had him there!'

He's right out of reach of the knife, thought Ronan with relief.

Then Mary Ann decided the scene needed a new twist. She seized the pig by his tail, pulling hard enough to give him a fright, but not hard enough to stop him. The pig leaped forward like a giant pink porpoise. With one bound, he was up the steps and amongst the greenery. His powerful jaws reached out and grabbed an expensive potted plant. He was getting frightened, though, with all the noise and the shouting. One end of him chewed the potted plant, clay pot and all; but the other end of him did what alarmed pigs do, even in the best of company.

He deposited a large, steaming, smelly mess all over the carefully polished shoes of Mr Vesey Fitzgerald.

The crowd loved that. There were shouts of, 'Vote for the pig!' 'He's better than Vesey Fitzgerald any day!' 'What about a bit of bacon for the tenants' dinner, Mr Fitzgerald?' The newspaper reporters – even the reporter from the *London Times* – tried to scribble in their notebooks while holding their aching sides and wiping tears of laughter from their cheeks.

Ronan watched the scene with narrowed eyes. He saw Mary Ann glance towards the false priest, estimating the distance; then, neatly sidestepping the smelly mess on the ground, she efficiently drove the pig right up against the man's legs. There was a startled yell and a shouted word that no priest should ever use, then a ringing sound; the pretend priest, leaping back, had dropped something in his haste.

John Steele bent down, picked it up and stared at it. He had a knife in his hand – a long, sharp, wicked-looking knife. Suddenly the crowd fell silent.

'Oh, look!' called Mary Ann, her clear voice ringing to the outer corners of the square. 'That priest isn't a priest at all. He's an assassin. He's trying to kill Daniel O'Connell!'

There was an ugly roar from the crowd. Everyone surged forward – and then they stopped. The 'priest' had rapidly wrenched the knife from John Steele; with his other hand, he had grabbed a fistful of Mary Ann's curls. He held the knife to her throat.

'Take one step towards me,' he shouted, 'and I cut her throat.'

Everyone froze – except one man. Ronan could see his father, right over at the corner of the square, beginning to work his way quietly and cautiously towards the courthouse steps. He was trying to get behind Smith and Mary Ann, Ronan guessed. Now was the time for the backup troops. He looked at Bruno's large head, just beside his chair, and said quietly into one of the big floppy ears, 'Bruno, find Mary Ann!'

Bruno shot forward, through the crowd, and mounted the courthouse steps at a speed that made him look even bigger than he really was. When he reached the top of the steps, something about the tense atmosphere seemed to affect him, and he began to bark. The huge, deep bark reverberated off the tall buildings around the square, so that it sounded as if a hundred giant dogs were barking. Then Bruno advanced on the assassin, his lip curled in a snarl and his bark changing to a low, thunderous growl.

At the sound of the growl, Smith glanced around. He saw a dog the size of a man, advancing on him, teeth bared, ready to attack. He whipped the knife away from Mary Ann's throat and held it steadily in front of him, at the level of the dog's jaws.

Warily Bruno circled around him. The thunder of his growls intensified, but some instinct warned him to keep clear of the knife. Despite his bulk, he moved quickly and lightly, like a boxer in a ring. He gave a quick, short bark of defiance and rushed at the assassin's leg.

In that instant, Michael sprang up the steps, seized Mary Ann in his arms, and carried her back down into the square, while Smith was still keeping the dog at bay with his deadly knife.

'Why don't you shoot him?' shouted Daniel O'Connell to the soldiers in the background. 'Go on, shoot him, before he kills the dog.'

The soldiers looked at their commanding officer. No sign was made. None of them moved.

An ugly grin came over Daniel O'Connell's face. 'So that's the way of it,' he sneered. 'He's under someone's orders, is he? Come on, lads, we'll take him ourselves! Call the dog off, Jack.'

The crowd surged forward, most of them waving heavy blackthorn sticks. A giant of a man from Kilfenora brought his stick down smartly on Smith's wrist, forcing him to drop the knife. Jack Carmody plunged up the steps and grabbed Bruno by the collar. The assassin lashed out with a tremendous kick that almost broke the jaw of the man who had bent to pick up the knife, then dived through the crowd of Vesey Fitzgerald's supporters, took the steps in one splendid leap and was off running down Church Street before anyone could recover their senses.

At that exact moment, Jimmy decided that, with everyone's attention on the escaping man, it might be the right time for him to regain possession of his pig, which was still on the courthouse steps, happily munching on the greenery. He had a dim idea that a landlord as powerful as Mr Vesey Fitzgerald might be able to do terrible things to the owner of a pig that had made such a mess of his nice shiny shoes. Visions of prison, whipping, or even hanging flashed through Jimmy's mind. Cautiously he crept forward. No one was looking at him; everyone was shouting, and nearly everyone had started to run down Church Street.

Jimmy raced up the steps, bent down and grabbed the string dangling from the pig's rear leg. He thought he might be able to get the pig away quietly; but the pig, sensing a loss of the liberty that he had found so exciting, gave a scream of anger. It sounded so like a human scream that the people nearby turned to look at Jimmy. In his embarrassment, Jimmy fumbled and dropped the string.

The pig didn't hesitate. With a leap almost as impressive as Smith's, he jumped the steps and set off, tearing down Church Street, squealing loudly. The people parted, falling back slightly to allow him through. In a moment, the pig was the leader of the crowd chasing the assassin.

'Arrest that man!' shouted Daniel O'Connell angrily to the soldiers and policemen grouped at the side of the square. They looked back uneasily, glancing at their commanding officers from the corners of their eyes.

At the sound of Daniel O'Connell's voice, Smith glanced over his shoulder. The captain of the soldiers made a reluctant gesture, and the regiment of soldiers charged across the square after him and began to run down Church Street. The assassin put on an extra burst of speed, but the pig, alarmed by the soldiers, also redoubled his pace.

Ronan watched tensely. Smith had to be caught. *If he's not caught now, he might come back and try again to kill Daniel O'Connell*, he thought. He had understood the sneer in Daniel O'Connell's voice. The soldiers weren't really trying to catch Smith. Why should they? Wasn't he one of them?

The assassin would probably have escaped if he had been wearing his soldier's uniform, but the long, clinging skirts of the priest's cassock hampered him. As he plunged forward, his foot caught in the hem of his skirt. He fell heavily, and the pig tumbled on top of him. In a moment, Daniel O'Connell and his friends were standing over him. Jimmy was right behind them; in one deft movement, he grabbed the string and hauled the pig away, back to where Ronan sat.

'Never ask me to let go of him again,' he said hoarsely. 'It's a good job my da isn't in Ennis today. The pig will have lost ten pounds of fat from all that running around.'

Ronan gave one glance at the immensely fat pig, but did not reply. He was straining his ears to hear what Daniel O'Connell was saying.

'I want this man committed for the next Assizes,' he was shouting. 'I have a hundred witnesses to the fact that he was behind me with a knife. And don't think you can quietly lose him, either; I'll be there in court myself, and I'll be a witness. I hope you're writing all this down, lads,' he shouted back to the reporters. 'Ye'll have a great story there.'

Ronan glanced at the reporters. Yes, they were all scribbling busily, though a few of them were still wiping tears of laughter from their faces. He sighed with satisfaction. That was all right, then: Daniel O'Connell would make sure that Smith was sent to prison.

Mary Ann had disentangled herself from Michael's arms and run over to stand proudly beside Ronan, a flush of triumph on her face. Ronan smiled at her. *Weren't we clever?*

She smiled back at him. She knew that he had appreciated every moment of her performance. There was no need for words between them.

Ronan suddenly stopped smiling. *But what about the men I heard in the hotel?* he thought. *The men who disguised Smith and sent him to stick a knife in Daniel O'Connell. What about them?*

He looked around the square, stretching his neck as far as he could. Most people were looking at Daniel

O'Connell and at the policemen who were reluctantly handcuffing Smith; but at the back of the square two figures were quietly stealing away, with furtive glances over their shoulders. Ronan knew who they were. One was the yellow-faced landlord who had threatened Ronan with his whip; the other was his friend, the handsome one with the cold eyes. Somehow Ronan was certain: these were the men whom he had heard plotting Daniel O'Connell's death.

'Mary Ann!' he screamed. 'Look! Men!'

Mary Ann had been feeling that sudden let-down that comes to every actress after a successful performance. She was no longer at the centre of the stage, and no one was looking at her any more. She didn't quite under-stand what Ronan meant, but she followed the direction of his eyes and immediately jumped at the opportunity to direct the crowd's attention onto herself once more.

'Mr O'Connell,' she shouted, pointing at the corner of the square. 'Look at those men!'

The effect was electrifying. There was a roar like an angry bull from the handcuffed Smith. 'If you're going to arrest me,' he yelled, 'arrest them too! Arrest those two men. They're the ones who paid me to do it.'

The crowd were as keen as Mary Ann to set the action moving again. 'Catch hold of them!' 'Don't let them go!' 'Give them a wallop with your stick, Willie Pat!' 'Watch that whip of his, Michael Joe!' Advice, orders and howls of laughter filled the square until the two landlords were dragged over to the police sergeant, who reluctantly took them into his charge.

'And you make sure they appear in court, too,' said Daniel O'Connell through gritted teeth, 'or, by God, I'll go before King George himself with the whole story. And now, lads,' he continued, his voice going back to its usual good-natured tone, 'don't let's forget that we have an election to finish and a result to hear.'

Gradually the crowd settled down again, and Daniel O'Connell and his friends returned to the steps in front of the courthouse. The Returning Officer cleared his throat and stepped forward.

'Mr William Vesey Fitzgerald – nine hundred and eighty-two votes,' he said. There was a wild cheer from the crowd. They knew what was coming. Several of the landlords turned pale.

'Mr Daniel O'Connell – two thousand and eighty-two votes. And,' the Returning Officer continued rapidly, 'by the power entrusted to me by His Majesty's Government, I hereby declare the said Daniel O'Connell to be returned as Member of Parliament for County Clare.'

There had been dead silence in the square while the Returning Officer read the results, but now the air exploded with noise. Anyone who had a tin whistle blew it, drums were beaten, but even their sound was drowned by the shouts of joy that burst from two thousand throats.

'Three cheers for Daniel O'Connell,' shouted Jack Carmody, and Ronan joined in the cheers almost as loudly as anyone else.

'You'd better take that pig of yours off home now, Jimmy,' said Jack Carmody, when all the cheering had died down and the people were starting to go back to their towns and villages.

Jimmy looked at him apprehensively, but there was still an ear-to-ear grin on Jack's broad red face; and all the other ladies and gentlemen still seemed amused when they looked at the pig. Jimmy relaxed.

'And here's a guinea for you,' added Daniel O'Connell. 'You and the pig have done me a great service today – and given me the best laugh I've had in a while,' he added, chuckling again at the thought of what the pig had done to Vesey Fitzgerald and to Smith.

'A guinea!' gasped Mary Ann.

Ronan said nothing. Jimmy obviously had never seen a guinea before – he was looking dubiously at the gold piece in his hand – but Ronan didn't feel like enlightening him. He was filled with jealousy and rage. Why should Jimmy get a guinea and he get nothing? He was the one who had spotted the disguised soldier; he was the one who had plotted the whole scene; he was the one who had saved Daniel O'Connell.

'Me!' he said, loudly and indignantly, to Mary Ann. *Tell them about me. Tell them what I did. Tell them that it was all my idea!* His pale face flushed with the effort of trying to convey his meaning.

'Not now, Ronan,' whispered Mary Ann. He could see in her eyes that she was planning something. It was hard for him to wait – he was used to people running to get him what he wanted, as soon as he wanted it – but he had grown up a lot during their few days in Ennis. He understood what Mary Ann meant. Everything had to be right when she told the whole story. He would explain it all to her, and she would tell Daniel O'Connell. Then maybe Daniel O'Connell would give him a guinea, too – maybe even two guineas.

Chapter Twelve

'That was clever,' said Mary Ann appreciatively. She and Ronan were alone in the stable. Ronan was supposed to be having a sleep; that evening he and his father were going to have dinner with Daniel O'Connell, his friends, and the parish workers. Ronan teased Mary Ann about the fact that she wasn't going, but she just tossed her head and told him no lady would join a gentlemen's dinner in a public hotel.

'Anyway,' she added, 'I'd much rather be the waitress. It's like being in a play, and all the gentlemen give me presents. You'd better go to sleep now, or you'll be too tired for the dinner.'

But Ronan couldn't sleep until he had told Mary Ann the whole story of how he had overheard the whispered words in Carmody's Hotel, and how he had recognised the soldier with the odd scar across his eyebrow, even in his priest disguise. He said nothing about Ned; that wasn't important any more. He was sure that Ned had had nothing to do with Smith. He had just played a stupid trick that had gone wrong.

'You . . . tell . . . Daniel O'Connell?' he asked anxiously.

Mary Ann ruffled his hair. 'I'll tell him,' she promised. 'Now you have a sleep. You want to be in good form for the dinner. Da's going to give you a bath later, and Mrs Carmody gave me a lovely shirt for you. It belonged to her son when he was young, and it's got all lace and ruffles on it. You'll be the finest gentleman there when we have you dressed.'

'You stay,' ordered Ronan, closing his eyes. He didn't want to be left on his own. He was still a little nervous. He would be glad to go back to Drumshee, he thought sleepily. He would be safe there.

★ ★ ★

Dinner was splendid. The table was covered with more food than Ronan had ever seen. He couldn't eat much — he was too excited — and his father didn't press him; but he loved watching all the gentlemen eat and listening to them talk. Everyone was talking about Daniel O'Connell.

'He'll wake up the House of Parliament, over there in London,' said one worker from Kilrush.

'He'll be the man to get tenant rights for the Irish,' said Father Murphy to another priest.

'We'll see Catholics being able to be doctors and judges soon,' said one of the shopkeepers.

'A terrible man to spend money, though,' whispered Mr Shields. 'He'd spend his last penny if his wife didn't keep a close eye on him. Do you know, I saw him take a hundred-pound note out of his pocket and give it to one of his poor relations down in Kerry! When he saw me looking, he just winked at me and whispered, "Don't tell Mrs O'Connell, whatever you do!" That wasn't the first time he did that, either.'

'A hundred pounds is nothing to the gentry,' said another man. Ronan didn't know his name, though he knew his face. 'They say Mr Vandeleur, a landlord from east Clare, spent that much on bribes at this election.'

A hundred pounds is nothing to the gentry; the words rang in Ronan's mind over and over again, like the church bell on Sundays. If only his father had a hundred pounds, they could all go off to France. . . . He looked at Mary Ann, who was darting in and out, serving everyone so quickly and neatly that anyone would imagine she had been doing it all her life. Ronan's eyes signalled to her, and she came across to him instantly.

'Do you want some more to eat?' she whispered.

Ronan shook his head. 'Tell,' he ordered, holding her eyes with his own and directing his gaze at Daniel O'Connell.

'Not now, Ronan,' Mary Ann whispered back, and in a moment she was at the other side of the table, removing a used plate and slipping a clean one into its place. Ronan fumed silently, but there was nothing he could do; he had to wait until Mary Ann found the right moment.

He didn't have long to wait, however. There was a sudden lull in the conversation as Daniel O'Connell, who had been helping himself to some of the plum tart that Mary Ann was serving, laid down his spoon and said in his booming voice, 'Well, now, Mary Ann, how did that pig get loose and get up on the courthouse steps? What happened? Tell us all about it.'

Mary Ann gave a quick glance around the table. Everyone had been served with plum tart, and every eye was on her. Ronan held his breath.

'Would you like to hear the whole story?' asked Mary Ann, her clear voice filling the room and her glance including everyone at the table.

'Wait a moment,' said Daniel O'Connell. 'Jack, a cherry brandy for everyone, and then we'll all hear it. I had a feeling there was a story behind that.'

Da's right, thought Ronan. *Daniel O'Connell is a clever man*.

Mary Ann waited until the last glass was filled. She took a step to one side, so that every eye could see her, and folded her hands in front of her frilly white apron.

'The story really begins earlier today, when Ronan was stolen from outside the hotel and left in his chair down by the river,' she began. 'Well, when he was down there he saw the soldiers crossing the bridge. Now, Ronan always notices everything. If he saw a feather in the yard, he could tell you which duck it came from. So, as he was looking at these soldiers, he noticed that one of them had a scar across his eyebrow. And it was great good luck for Mr O'Connell that he noticed that.'

She paused. Everyone was staring at her. One man who had picked up a cream jug held it suspended in the air, and then put it down without adding any cream to his tart. No one was eating; no one was drinking. Everyone was held by Mary Ann's gaze.

'So when Ronan saw that very same scar, those very same eyes, that very same man standing behind Mr O'Connell – not wearing a soldier's uniform now, but dressed as a priest – he knew immediately that something bad was going to happen. He saw the knife in the man's sleeve. He told me, and he shouted to Jimmy to let go of the string on the pig's leg. I managed to get the pig right up onto the courthouse steps, and then Ronan told Bruno to fetch me. And that was how it happened – how Ronan saved Daniel O'Connell's life.'

Mary Ann came across the room and put her arm around Ronan's thin shoulders. Still she held her audience with her eyes, and still no one moved.

'Ronan was very brave,' she went on softly, but her voice still reached to the furthermost corner of the room. 'Yesterday, when he was by himself in the little reading-room, he overheard the plot to kill Daniel O'Connell. The men guessed that he knew, and he heard them planning to push his chair in the river. Even then, he didn't tell anyone; he just went on looking and listening. He only told me about it this evening. You see, before we ever came to Ennis, he had decided that he was the best person to be the secret spy from Drumshee – and he knew that the most important thing was to look after Daniel O'Connell, no matter how much danger he was in himself.'

There was a silence; then Jack Carmody blew his nose and mopped his eyes with a navy-spotted white silk handkerchief. One or two people cleared their throats. Daniel O'Connell looked steadily at Ronan, and there was admiration and respect in his eyes. Ronan looked proudly back at him. Michael's hand tightened convulsively on Ronan's arm, and Ronan knew that he was upset. *It's a pity Da was here*, Ronan thought; *things like that upset him*. Nevertheless, he continued to look at Daniel O'Connell, who got up from his chair and came around the table to them.

'Thank you for telling us the story so well, Mary Ann,' he said gently. 'Ronan, I owe you my life, and I will never forget your courage and your cleverness. Michael,' he added, 'you must let me give Ronan a present, something to reward him.'

Money, thought Ronan. *Lots of money for going to France!* He looked at Mary Ann. She would be able to ask – she would be able to do it well. . . . But Mary Ann avoided his gaze. He would have to do it himself.

'Hundred pounds,' he said eagerly. The words shot from him like a bullet from a gun.

'Ronan!' said Michael, turning the colour of beetroot. Mary Ann gasped, her face turning as red as her father's, and stifled a giggle by pressing her hands to her mouth. Ronan looked at them both and felt his face going red.

'You must excuse him, Mr O'Connell,' said Michael. 'He's tired; he doesn't know what he's saying. I'll take him away now. It's time we were going, anyway; we have a long journey ahead of us.'

Ronan felt terrible. Words were so difficult for him that he had the habit of saying exactly what was in his mind. Mary Ann didn't do that, he knew. He should have left it to her. She would have managed better. Now he had spoiled everything and was being taken away in disgrace. He took a long breath and tried to control his violently jerking body, but only a crowing sound came out.

'Wait a minute, son,' said Daniel O'Connell gently. 'Don't upset yourself. Now what do you think, every-one? Is my life worth a hundred pounds?'

'Yes!' roared all the gentlemen.

'A thousand pounds,' said Gorman McMahon.

'Well, there you are, Ronan,' said Daniel O'Connell. 'I'll give you a hundred pounds now, and I'll owe you nine hundred until I make a bit more money. Is that a bargain?'

He put his hand in his inside pocket, took out his wallet and pulled out a large banknote. He leaned over and tucked it into Ronan's pocket.

'No, Mr O'Connell,' said Michael, almost as distressed as his son. 'Don't do that. Give him a shilling and he'll be happy. He doesn't know what he's saying.'

'He knows the value of money, and he knows the value of my life,' said Daniel O'Connell seriously. 'The boy is quite right.'

Ronan drew in another few deep breaths. He was still gripped by violent spasms, but he made a superhuman effort.

'Da . . . moneybox . . . France . . . sun . . . make chairs . . . Mary Ann,' he said. *Tell him about all our plans*, his eyes implored Mary Ann. *Tell him how Da wants to go to France and make furniture – tell him how the sun helps the pain in my back – tell him how you want to be an actress.*

Gradually he managed to relax as Mary Ann told the story of the dream they shared, of the moneybox that filled so slowly, and once again tears came to the eyes of several of her audience.

'Ronan didn't really mean to ask for money,' she ended simply, her cheeks still pink with embarrassment. 'He finds it so hard to talk that sometimes he says a thought, not just thinks it.'

Daniel O'Connell smiled at her. 'Well, the world might be a better place if we all did that,' he said. 'And, Mary Ann, don't let anyone talk you out of being an actress. I can see that you'll be magnificent.'

Ronan began to feel better. Gradually his breathing eased. Daniel O'Connell wheeled his chair to the top of the table and stood beside him. Everyone looked up at the great man and the crippled boy.

'Well, gentlemen,' said Daniel O' Connell, 'we've drunk many toasts this evening, but now I'll ask you to fill your glasses and stand for the most important toast of them all.'

Everyone stood, glasses in hand, as Daniel O'Connell raised his glass and said, 'To Ronan, the secret spy from Drumshee!'

And those words, and the sight of all the white-shirted gentlemen toasting him, and the roar of their cheers, stayed with Ronan for the rest of his life.

Epilogue

en months later, on the first day of May in the year 1829, Ronan, Mary Ann and their father Michael set sail for France. The little farm of Drumshee was left to John, who had just got married to Nora Dooley. John and Nora lived there until the days of the terrible Famine of 1845. They had four children: Martin was born in 1832; the twins, Deirdre and Fiona – twins ran in the McMahon family – were born in 1833; and Daniel, the youngest, was born in 1835.

When Ronan, Mary Ann and Michael reached France, they made their way to the small village of Rozay, near Orléans, south of Paris. There Michael joined his sister-in-law Aimée and her husband Jean, and he began to make beautiful furniture for rich French people. Much of the old furniture in the French chateaux had been destroyed during the French Revolution of 1789, but now the country was prosperous and big new country houses were being built. Michael and Jean prospered, and Ronan was happy advising and criticising. The French climate, with its long hot summers and the dry cold of its winters, made him feel much better, and a French doctor gave him medicine that helped his spasms when they were too severe.

As Ronan grew older and a little stronger, he began to recognise the truth of what his father had said to him in Carmody's Hotel. He understood how much Mary Ann had done for him and he began to feel grateful to her. They were always great friends and Ronan began to feel proud of Mary Ann, just as Mary Ann was always proud of Ronan.

Mary Ann did become an actress. She was the first of the family to learn French, and soon she could chatter away as if she had been born in France. Michael did so well in the furniture business that he was able to pay for singing and dancing lessons for her. By the time she was seventeen, she was already appearing in plays, and by the time she was twenty-one she was on the stage in Paris. She did get married, but not to Ned Dooley – and the tale of her life, her successes and her marriage is another story.

SOON TO BE RELEASED . . .

**The new style BOOK 6 in the gripping
Drumshee Timeline Series**

TITANIC VOYAGE FROM
DRUMSHEE

Fourteen-year old Kitty is leaving Drumshee. She is crossing the Atlantic
Ocean to America on board the greatest ship ever built – the Titanic.

Δs nursemaid to Lady Victoria Fitzgerald's niece and nephew, Tabitha
and Robert, Kitty revels in the splendour of the magnificent ship.
Meeting the other passengers, especially the handsome John, adds to the
sense of adventure.

Kitty is having so much fun she decides to ignore her grandmother's
warnings that anyone who takes the Drumshee necklace out of
Drumshee is looking for trouble. Anyway Kitty is sure that nothing is
going to go wrong.

★ ★ ★

Also from WOLFHOUND PRESS . . .

BOOK 12 in the Drumshee Timeline Series

DARK DAYS AT
DRUMSHEE

Alys just wants to enjoy her new job at Lemeanah Castle and have fun
riding her beautiful pony Silky. But these are dangerous times at
Drumshee. The English Royalists have joined forces with the Irish to
fight Oliver Cromwell's soldiers. One dark night Alys overhears three
soldiers talking on a dark road . . . .

Who is plotting to kill Conor O'Brien, the master of Lemeanah
Castle?

Is it haughty Colonel Roberts or Alys's own cousin Sir Charles?

Even worse, is it handsome, laughing Francis?

Will Alys and Silky reach Conor and warn him – before it's too late?

COMING SOON . . .

BOOK 14 in the Drumshee Timeline Series

Banished from Drumshee

'And I took his body in my arms, and I carried him up to the top of Mount Callan.

And I laid him in the shallow grave that I had hollowed out of the stony soil.

And then I shovelled the earth over him and hid him forever.'

I carried over a heavy flagstone and placed it on the mound.

And with my knife I carved these words.

'Here lies Conan, the fierce and turbulent.'

Who was Conan? Why was he called 'fierce and turbulent'? How did he die? Who buried him?

In the Eight Century turmoil of warring tribes, love, jealousy, blackmail and revenge, Conan's story unfolds. He entangles his foster brother, Columba, and the beautiful Sorcha in a terrifying adventure that will change all their lives forever.

★ ★ ★

Orders or Enquiries to:
Wolfhound Press
An Imprint of Merlin Publishing
16 Upper Pembroke Street, Dublin 2, Ireland
publishing@merlin.ie
www.merlin-publishing.com